MW01180550

Rapunzel and Thorn-proof Tires

When I swim, I think. It is such a solitary activity, swimming. Oh, being in the pool isn't necessarily solitary. There are usually a number of people standing in the water like dinosaurs. They visit and enjoy the sun while lounging in the cool water, and I thread among them, like a fish, or, more accurately, like a snake. I like to keep my head above the water. I try to be inconspicuous because I know that when someone is obviously trying to swim in a pool full of people who are just standing in the water, more or less in the way of the swimmer, well, they must feel like the swimmer is annoyed with them. They must feel that way, because I would feel that way, and I would probably get out of the swimmer's way, maybe even get out of the pool altogether, if I were just standing there visiting, which I could do just as well while sitting in a lawn chair beside the pool...

Anyway, when I swim, I think. I guess I imagine things, really. I thread in and out among the dinosaurs and, while half listening to their conversations, I have deep thoughts.

I don't know what other people who swim think about. One time I was staying in a motel, and I had the pool all to myself, and I was swimming back and forth the length of the medium sized pool, enjoying my imaginings, when a young man burst into the pool room, dropped his towel, eyed me a moment, then dove in and rapidly splashed back and forth, twice or more to my one time. He kept that up for, oh, maybe ten minutes, before, all tired out, he pulled himself up onto the edge of the pool, dripping and shaking the water from his hair like a dog. I continued my slow swim across the water, which finally was calming itself after the young man's busy thrashing, and, as I smoothly slid past him, I said, "I like to go slowly. You go so quickly across. Do you enjoy that?"

And he said, "Oh yes! I like to go as fast as I can, especially after a rough day or if I've been traveling. As fast as I can."

And I laughed. I said, "I like to see people who enjoy swimming. I love just moving slowly through the water though!"

He laughed again. "That's not me! I love to go as fast as I can!" And he stood up, smiled as he nodded to me, and then went on his way. I wish I had asked him what he thought about as he swam. I wonder if he thought about anything beyond his racing heart and his straining muscles and his panting breath. Well, he wasn't in the water very long, so it wouldn't have been a very well-crafted thinking, anyway.

I know what the dinosaurs think about when they are in the water…at least I know what they talk about, because I hear what they say as I glide past them. Sometimes I even make a comment, but only when I feel confident that no one will feel like I was eavesdropping, which is what I was doing, of course. But usually I am deep in my own thoughts and their light chatter isn't where I am, and so I say nothing. I just swim as unobtrusively as possible and use my Mona Lisa smile to mask my sometimes tumultuous thoughts and imaginings.

******

When I swim, sometimes I think about fairy tales and folk tales. I think about my life, and about fairy tales that I loved or hated as a child. When I have been asked to name my favorite fairy tale, I often have said the name of the first fairy tale I think of…and that has always been 'Rapunzel'. Not a favorite, though! I hated that fairy tale as a child. Still, oddly enough, for years, in journal groups, in library groups, in child-development classes, in literature classes; when asked for a favorite fairy tale, I have automatically said, "Rapunzel" and then instantly have been annoyed with myself, because I remember that as a child, I so hated that fairy tale that I couldn't even read it to the end.

Reading. I don't think that my parents read much to me when I was little. My grandfather read to me…but he read Dickens and Mark Twain, more for himself, I think than to entertain me. He read to me from whatever he was reading. I usually got the middle of the chapter, just part of the story, and then I had to fill in the missing parts on my own.

I was always told that I had taught myself to read…somehow. Someone must have read to me more frequently than I remember, or how could I have taught myself? At any rate, there is a whole story about my reading ability. I started into first grade when I was five years old, and I was already reading to myself at that time. When my mother and I went to meet the first grade teacher, Miss Horn, my mother tried to tell her that I could already read. Miss Horn said, rather curtly, "No, she can't."

My mother said, "But she can read. She can read for you now. Ask her to read. I've even brought a book so that she can read to you."

Ah, that was my mother's mistake, because after I had read some from the book which my mother provided, Miss Horn simply insisted that I had memorized that particular book. She insisted that I wasn't reading it. She said that I had learned it from having it read to me. At any rate, when we left the terrible, terrorizing Miss Horn, I was not feeling very sure of myself anymore, and my mother was furious. It didn't help me much that as soon as we were out of Miss Horn's room, my mother grabbed my arm, leaned over me in a somewhat menacing way and said, "I don't know if you can really read or not, but if you can't, don't you ever let Miss Horn know it!" And then we marched home.

I was reading, though. And surely Miss Horn figured that out. I spent most of the first grade day-dreaming while Miss Horn worked with other children. I mainly remember sitting at a little table in the back of the room with number tiles. I think I was supposed to be 'learning my numbers', but what I was doing was making up stories for them. I remember 5 was an all-round good guy, and 7 was a fair-weather sort of friend and 9 was just plain naughty. 1 and 2 were just babies and you couldn't really expect much of them. Numbers 3, 4, 6, and 8 were the variables, though, sometimes good and reliable, sometimes not. I don't remember the actual situations that they struggled through, but I do remember that Miss Horn made me go outside for recess and put them in their box before I was ready. And I hated the games we played at recess. And I read my brother's school books to him when we got home, because he was far-sighted and that had not been discovered very quickly, and he had trouble with reading even though he was several years older than I was.

But back to 'Rapunzel'. At a rather early age I read the traditional fairy tales from a copy of Grimm's fairy tales that had been given to me for my birthday. After I read a few of those stories that even then had been popularized by Disney, I branched out to read the others, and that is when I discovered 'Rapunzel'. I tried to read it. I managed to 'suspend my disbelief' as I read the part about the special plant that the mother craved, and I even managed to endure the part about the witch taking the little baby and raising her in a tower. The long hair part was, I realized, obviously magical, as I was the possessor of a head of wispy straw that I knew, even then, could and would never grow very long and would certainly never be strong enough to use as a rope ladder. Actually, my hair was so fragile that it broke even when it was being combed and never really got thick or long enough for a stringy ponytail until I was a teenager…that hair stuff was make-believe for certain.

But the boy who fell and got his eyes scratched out… that is where I stopped reading. And I never actually read that story to the end until I was, maybe, forty years old. All those years I thought that the boy was blinded forever and that Rapunzel, well, she was lost in time…no hair, so things couldn't just go on as they had been, and so, I believed, that she was still miserable and wandering forlornly in a desert somewhere or, maybe, if the witch had relented, that she was stuck back in that tower.

I hated that story. Yet every time someone asked me what my favorite fairy tale had been when I was a child, I would say, "Rapunzel" without the slightest hesitation. Guilt and shame would wash over me! I would feel that I had cheated somehow; that I had given a wrong answer. Why would I immediately mention a story I hadn't even read? A story I hated with such strong feelings? It irritated me, but I never, never took the time to really think about it.

When I was forty or so, and I had read Bruno Bettelheim and Joseph Campbell and Jack Zipes, I finally decided that I needed to read 'Rapunzel'…all the way through. I had listened in on the retellings of favorite fairy tales that my own children had chosen to tell each other. I certainly understood that fairy tales are magical and special to each person. I could even see why each of my children particularly loved their especially chosen stories. And I knew that I hated 'Rapunzel' with all my heart, and it was still the only story that came to mind when I was asked to quickly name a fairy tale.

...And also, when I was forty or so, after years of standing patiently in the water while holding up one child or another and then carefully teaching those water-soaked children to swim, I, myself, had started to swim again, and, therefore, I had started to think.

******

Of course there are many different versions of 'Rapunzel', including the more recent movie, 'Tangled', version. But, at that time, when I decided, at last, to read the story completely, I chose to read from my own old edition of the Grimm's stories. I wanted to face the ending I had avoided for so many years.

I had to find that particular book first, but I knew that I still had it. My mother had found it years before, left in a drawer in my old room, and she had given it back to me in a box with some of my other childhood books that she had saved. I had put that book high on a shelf, thinking to myself that the book was too fragile for my children's rough use. Perhaps, also, I thought those stories were too harsh for them, although I knew that they all had read the same tales in their own books and in books from the library, and I knew that they had read and seen even harsher things in their media filled lives.

I remember what I felt when I finally read to the end of the story in that old copy of Grimm's Fairy Tales. Healing tears? Why hadn't I imagined that? And there was so much more! Deep, deep stuff. Babies? Survival? Reunion? Things were happening in that story about which I had had no idea. How was it that I had gotten stuck in the middle of the story, and I had to wait for almost half a century before I could deal with it and explore the ending? And how was it that my own story mirrored that hated fairy tale in so many ways in the deepest places and also in some very obvious, on-the-surface, places. The themes and threads of that story were in place in my life and, although I fought it and denied it, some part of me knew, even as a young child reading that fairy tale for the first time, that that particular story had a message for me. A piercing of the heart, a thorn in an eye.

To begin, I grew up in a small town in eastern Indiana. My family came to this town as strangers—outsiders—if you will. My grandparents had been prominent people in neighboring Ohio, but a compendium of tragedies had beset them, and they had felt compelled to leave their well-appointed abode and, therefore, abandon their stain-free and well respected reputation and standing…at least that is what I was told. I later learned that my grandfather had lost almost all of his savings in the crash of '29 and, then had been swindled out of his interest in a manufacturing business which he had nurtured into success, but which failed almost immediately after he lost his case in court…and then my grandparent's youngest son, my father's younger brother, the fair-haired boy of the family…not the silly, funny, clever, yet foolish middle son who was my father…died suddenly of peritonitis.

My father, a musician with no head for business, an elf of a man who had chosen to attend a college because of the pretty girls he saw there and the reputation it had for being a party school, a man who had always been the family jester, had been overwhelmed with grief at the loss of his brother. It had been doubly painful because when the news of his brother's death had reached his parents, they had at first thought that my father had died…everyone in the town had thought that…and when everyone, including his parents, learned that the younger son was the one who had died…well, my father realized that his brother had had a special place in the family and now my father's role in this family had been changed in a way he had never imagined.

It wasn't that his parents and siblings hadn't loved him as much as they had his younger brother…it was that he hadn't been as important. He hadn't been taken as seriously. He had been more expendable. My grandmother was bereaved beyond consolation by the loss of this youngest brother, this favorite child of hers. And so the family was shattered. ..for a while. They walked together in awkward silence. My father even arranged secretly to have his healthy appendix removed so that he could assure his mother that no such fate as had happened to his brother would happen to him. He would always be there. He would fit himself into his brother's too tight shoes to please his parents. Slowly, the family began to restructure itself. The older sisters, already married and off with their own families, and the oldest son, established on his mission of making a name for himself in business and caring for his growing family, were not so involved in this process. My grandfather, angry and saddened but refusing to be beaten by these events, and his bereaved wife sold their well-appointed home and moved with their remaining son, my father, across the border into Indiana.

They bought a simple older home…not so grand as the home they had left, but no one here knew that…and they paid in cash…very important when you move to a new town. My grandfather bought a small business, again with cash, and set my father up as a businessman. My father, the musician who wanted to write music for the big dance bands, who daydreamed about having his own dance band, who loved to be thought of as a scamp and a tease, became a Western Auto man.

And I was the Western Auto man's daughter. I wasn't the first and only child. I was the second child, the one that clinched the end of my father's dreams. He wasn't a particularly good businessman as you might guess, and it was all he could do, even with my grandfather's help, to keep the business going well enough to pay the bills for both my grandparents and for his own little family, for my father married my mother soon after the move, and then my brother was born and finally, myself. Of course, I didn't know all this when I was little. I just felt it in the background, like sometimes you can feel the tremor of the coming train when you stand on the station platform, waiting.

My grandparent's house in Indiana had become my parent's home also by the time I was born. At first my parents had had their own apartment, but my grandparents had taken turns getting ill--from the very first night of my parents' honeymoon (which was then at first curtailed but finally put off forever), until my mother finally conceded that it would just be easier to live in an apartment above my grandparents than to continuously have to spend time at their house caring for them and then try to return to take care of her own little place. Perhaps money had something to do with the decision... And so we all lived together separately.

The house had a huge yard which was divided into two large segments. The first backyard was my domain. It had a cherry tree and a huge old persimmon tree. The once extensive grape arbor immediately behind the house had been reduced to provide shade for the patio as well as grapes for eating, and, close by, there was a marvelous little summer kitchen that had been converted into a summer 'guest house' with bunk beds for my brother and me built into the wall by my clever, creative father, and a wonderful screen door that I loved to slam.

The second backyard was the garden. It was fenced-in all the way around and took up much of the backyards of all the other people who lived in the houses that made up the rest of the block. I never thought about it. I just assumed that it was our family's right to have all of the land, all of the yard space. I usually didn't play in the garden yard itself. But I did play in the entryway to the garden. There was a little decorative gate and just inside were benches with a trellis up and over them which was covered by wisteria, and the trellis had a little wrought iron lamp hanging from the center of its overhead section. I liked to sit there on the benches and pretend.

My mother and my grandmother both had vegetable gardens which included the usual fare of green beans and peas and potatoes, turnips and parsnips as well as strawberry beds, rhubarb, black raspberry bushes, two apple trees, a pear tree, quince bushes and a tailored rose garden with a lovely arbor covered with climbing roses, and all of this profuse greenery hid from view most of the backsides of the other houses. It was secluded in the center of the town.

I knew that I lived upstairs, more or less in what other people would describe as an apartment, but other people didn't seem to know that. There were no locked doors between my grandparent's domain and my parent's apartment. We had separate kitchens and bathrooms, but we could use

14

each other's kitchens and bathrooms if we needed, and, as a child, I frequently needed to use my grandparent's bathroom because it was downstairs and who wants to scurry up a rickety flight of backdoor stairs to go to the bathroom? But there were different rules involved. No going into Grandmother's bathroom if you are muddy...no taking other people's children into Grandmother's bathroom...and so the boundaries were drawn, not unpleasantly, perhaps, but there. But other people seemed to think that I lived in a great big house with a great big yard and that meant that I came from a family that had great big money. And that we were great big happy, all the time.

I never once heard my grandmother or my grandfather talk about my young, dead uncle. His picture, a posthumous painting, was hung on the wall, and I was told who he had been ...but never told anything more. I remember commenting on his blonde hair. My father's hair was dark, and my grandparent's had grey hair. My brother had auburn red hair, but I had blonde hair, like my poor dead uncle. I would comment about that as I stared at his painting, but no one ever offered a loving memory of him. I quickly realized that no one was going to satisfy my curiosity about this handsome young man who smiled down to me from the confines of his gold-framed window hung high up on the wall.

My room was upstairs in an unheated room toward the front of the house. Both my brother and I slept in the room during our youngest days. My earliest memory is standing in my crib calling for my parents who were in an adjoining room, but they couldn't hear me because they had company and were playing music. My brother had to go and get them for me. I don't remember what happened next, I just remember how I felt when he left the room to get them, and I was completely alone! Sometimes the result of complaining is worse than the original problem. I doubt that I conceptualized that, but that sums up how I felt!

When I outgrew my crib, my father designed a way to divide our room into two rooms so we could have a bit more privacy and, also, a place for our toys and belongings that was our very own. He built bunk beds into the center of the room, but he enclosed one side on the lower bunk and then enclosed the other side on the upper bunk. My brother took the upper bunk and the front-of-the-house side of the room, and I was given the lower bunk and a window that looked out over the roof of the neighboring home and right on over to the Carnegie library which sat on the corner of our block. My father put in shelves for us along the walls, and he put in closets for our hanging clothes. The closets were small and dark, as I found out in the next few years, because my brother would tease me by pushing me into one of the closets and then holding the door shut until I promised not to tell on him. I quickly learned that if I would just conquer my fear of the dark and stay quiet, that he would open the door to check on me, and, if I were quick enough, I could push my way out. My brother wasn't mean. He was just older... and he hadn't learned that to exercise power over someone else is not really a useful way to get what you want.

Oddly enough, that simple barrier of an enclosed side to our bunk beds was a very effective way to divide the space. I can't really describe my brother's side of the room. I remember that he had some airplane models that he hung from the ceiling and that he had a little desk, and I remember that he had a large piece of plywood with his train tracks on it for his trains and that he kept that under the bunk beds. But I remember my side in great detail! I had a charcoal painting of a black horse decorating the end of my bunk enclosure and another print of a Tennessee Walking horse on the inside wall. I had my stuffed animals on the shelves and my books, as well as some of my special toys like my fairy tale figures. I had a set of tiny rubbery plastic figures; of the Three Little Pigs with hard plastic structures for each of their houses and a little mean looking wolf; of Cinderella, complete with a pumpkin shaped carriage and a prince as well as mice and horses and, of course a fairy godmother and poor Cinderella and rich Cinderella; and there were a huntsman, a grandmother, another wolf, and a little Red Riding Hood. But no Rapunzel.

I remember looking out of my tall, narrow upstairs window and watching the stars above the town. Towns weren't so lighted up back then. A person could see stars and could watch the moon come up. I loved to watch the stars, and I wished on that first star almost every night. I never got my wish. At least I never got the wish that I remember the best. I started to wonder if, perhaps, somewhere out of a different window, there was an earlier star that I wasn't seeing, and that That Star was the real wishing star.

As I got older I learned about the constellations, and I decided that I should learn where they were. It would be useful to know them, since I would be able to see stars from wherever I might be, and that way I could never be lost or alone. I would never wander in a desert. I could find my way back, even in the night! I discovered that one good view of the stars was from a balcony with white painted railings that held flower boxes that were filled with petunias all summer long. The balcony had been built above the big wrap-around porch on the front of the house. There was a door which led out to that balcony from the hall right outside my bedroom door. In the warm summer evenings I would creep out of my room and slip outside onto the open, fenced-in space, and then I would lie down on the warm tin floor covering and stare up into the sky. Sometimes I would wake up and feel stiff and cold and then I would creep back inside and into my room and would snuggle down under my covers.

I did learn about the constellations, or at least I learned the names of them from books and then I tried to find them in the sky. Some of them I probably did find, but others, well, I just called an arrangement of stars that looked to me to be the constellation, the same name that some ancient astronomer had given it. I had my own constellations, I fear, because some, that, as an adult I learned are only seen in the southern sky, were visible to me from that northeastern porch. But it didn't really matter.

And so my early days were filled with beautiful gardens bountifully producing fruits and vegetables so sweet and fresh that to this day I love parsnips and greens and fresh beans, and I remember the taste of tomatoes plucked from the vine and bitten and then the juices licked out before the flesh is devoured. And there isn't a fruit that I won't try, because I trust that they will taste like those grapes or those pears, and I even remember pleasantly the frost bitten persimmons, so smooth and sweet…not at all like the seedy, acerbic little nubs that pucker your mouth before the frost!

It was an Eden of sorts. And, as we all know, in every Eden there is a serpent. I didn't know there was a serpent, of course, although I could feel its presence, like the tremble of the ground before the train…

I loved swimming even then. I loved water. When I was just a few months old I had a terrible case of eczema. I had picked it up in the hospital soon after I was born, and it was persistent. I didn't sleep well. I was just a miserable baby, and I seemed to be allergic to everything. As the weather grew nicer after my winter birth, my parents began going to the lake. My father loved boats, and he and my mother had a small outboard runabout, which they enjoyed taking out for rides. They soon discovered that I would instantly fall asleep if I were in the boat, even with the roar of the engine and the slap of the bow as it came down hard on the water as it crossed waves. And when the ride was over I would stay asleep as long as they left me in the boat, moored to the dock. My mother thought it was the murmur of the water and the rocking motion…but whatever it was, they took advantage of it. That first summer, as miserable as I must have been, I spent quite a bit of time sleeping in that little boat.

As I grew older, I continued to be drawn to the water. Whenever we went for picnics, or went camping, I would wander off, and when my parents would look for me, they knew to look wherever there was water. My mother would laugh and say, "And there you would be, squatting by the water, digging in the mud, or just putting things into the water and watching the water swirl around!"

My mother told me that one time the other women noticed that I had wandered off. Apparently, I was a toddler, or at least my mother said that I was, and she told them, "Oh, I don't worry about her! She will be by the edge of the water, playing!"

And the other women said, "But she might fall into the lake!" I don't know what my mother said to that.

At any rate, I remember when I moved from being a non-swimming mud puppy to becoming a fish or, perhaps, an otter. My father was in the river working on the boat. Perhaps he was tinkering with the engine. At any rate he was in deeper water and was not close to where I was playing. I decided to see what he was doing, and so I started out toward him. Suddenly, my feet were swept backward and I was forward in the water. I flailed about, clamped my mouth shut and kicked my feet. The next thing I knew, my father lifted me out of the water and said, "You were swimming!" He carried me to the shore and put me in the shallow water again, but I pitched forward with my eyes and mouth squeezed shut, lifted my legs and began kicking again. My father showed me how to cup my hands to give my arms more strength in the water. Later he showed me how to take a breath, with my head held above the water by my flailing arms, and then how to move forward again with my head down closer to the water. I'm sure it wasn't a pretty sight, but I felt as though I had conquered the world.

Actually I remember other milestones of swimming. My father's sister, Gini, encouraged me to learn to dive deep into the water. She threw coins into a pool and watched as I struggled to reach them, deeper and deeper in the water. Diving underwater was hard for me because I was so naturally buoyant. "Let out your breath, and you will sink!" other people would say. Dutifully, I would exhale, but I didn't sink. I floated. Even my legs floated. To reach the bottom of the pool, I had to fight my buoyancy every second. If I didn't grab my treasure the first grab, I had to struggle to stay down in order to try again. Usually I popped up to the surface like a cork and then had to fight my way down again. When I took swimming lessons, diving underwater was, for me, the most dreaded part. I never learned a simple way to reach the bottom with grace. I was a surface skimmer, a water strider, perhaps.

A water strider. An insect. A little girl child digging in the mud can discover another world of life. I found a world of creatures. I found centipedes, dragonfly nymphs, damselflies, and sand fleas. Some of them bit me. When I swam, I would come across tiny creatures struggling in the water, and I would carry them to shore and put them in the sand to dry their wings and revive. My Aunt Gini called me "the insect rescue patrol", but she insisted that there were insects that needn't be rescued. I disagreed. I thought that all of them deserved to live out their tiny lives. I remember being stung by one frightened and ungrateful wasp and how I cried. I couldn't understand why it hadn't understood that I was trying to save its life. My aunt was there for that moment, and she explained that sometimes frightened things aren't thinking clearly and that little things see the world differently anyway. She patted baking soda on my swollen finger, and suggested to me that I learn which insects bite and sting, and then I would know which ones to rescue on a leaf instead of on my hand.

And so I tried to learn about insects. Insects became my passion. I had been observing them all that time I was squatting close to them and playing. I knew that ants walked in straight lines and followed one another right up the side of the old persimmon tree to a spot where sticky sap was oozing out…and I had watched those ants, in what seemed to be a never ending line, march right back down and follow each other down the mysterious hole in the little grey mound between the bricks in the walk. I had watched the slow moving bumble bees thread their way among my grandmother's flowers, and I had discovered that they had a nest under the eaves of the back porch. Because I wanted to see if their nest was similar to the tidy little nests that the mud wasps made, or the intricate nests of the paper wasps, I used a stick to pry away the latticework and instantly the bumble bees flew out, and I scampered down the rickety back steps, but they chased me and began to sting me.

One of them got under my shirt and stung me again and again. My screams brought my mother to my rescue and she chased off the bees that had surrounded me, but I was still screaming.

"They are gone", she said as she hurried me inside the house.

"No!" I cried. "One is still stinging me!" I insisted.

She lifted my shirt and found one last bee, busily stinging me. She killed it and then removed my shirt. She counted the swollen lumps and found that, altogether, I had thirteen stings. Many of them were under my shirt. She and my grandmother were puzzled. I didn't seem to be suffering any ill effects from the stings other than the swollen lumps. The baking soda paste they busily applied seemed to mollify me, but the number of bee stings under my shirt continued to puzzle them.

"I thought bees could only sting once and then they died!" my mother said.

"That's true, I'm certain", offered my grandmother. It was confounding to them. How many bees must I have had under my shirt?

I was more concerned to learn that the bees that had stung me were now dead. "Why would they sting me if that meant they would die?" I wanted to know. "I wasn't going to hurt them! Why did they decide to come out and sting me and then they die because of that. They could have waited and seen I wasn't bad!"

My grandmother tsked and scolded me, now that it seemed I was just going to be unreasonable and not dead. "Why were you bothering their house? Now we will have to get rid of their nest. I told your grandfather and your father that the bees were too close to the house, and they might become a nuisance, but they didn't do anything!" And she left to make a phone call.

My mother was still worried about the number of stings under my shirt. "How many bees do you think were under your shirt?" she asked.

I couldn't answer, of course. I had no idea. "I guess we have to count the bumps under where my shirt was," I offered.

My mother frowned. "Yes, but there are at least nine sting places under where your shirt was, mostly on your back, but a few on your side. How did all those bees get out from under your shirt so fast after stinging you?" she wondered.

My grandfather came home from the store. He said that my father would be home soon and would investigate the matter of the bee's nest. He was trying to be careful about what he said about killing the bees in front of me, but I knew he was really telling my grandmother and mother that my father was bringing home whatever was needed to get rid of the nest. I had ambivalent feelings. I felt it was unfair to the bees, but then, I realized that I was a little afraid of them now. They could be mean very quickly, and they didn't give a person a chance to explain.

My mother posed her question about the bee attack. How could so many bees get under my shirt and sting me and then get away so quickly. My grandfather looked at my shirt and then at the sting swellings. He could see that my little shirt was too small to hide so many bees, and, besides how could so many bees get under there and sting and get out! He, too, had heard that bees only sting once. "Did you have your shirt on?" he asked me.

I nodded and my mother came to my defense. "Oh yes," she said. "I had to take it off of her to find that last bee that was stinging her!"

"Well, maybe we need to look this up in the encyclopedia," He suggested.

And we did. First we learned that there is a big difference between bumble bees and honey bees. Honey bees usually can only sting once and then they fly off to die. Bumble bees, on the other hand, can sting again and again...and again and again. My mother and I had fought off the bees that were flying around. I might have even out run them, and they might have simply returned to their nest after I left their territory...But one of their fellow warriors/nest guardians had found her way under my shirt and had no idea that I was getting away from the nest, or, maybe, in her panic, trying to fly away, kept getting caught by my shirt, and so she kept stinging me every time she touched my skin. I felt that I should be glad she was dead, yet I had a strange feeling of compassion for her. After all, she had just been doing her job to protect the nest and then got trapped and felt terribly threatened. She and I were engaged in a life and death battle from her point of view, and now she was dead, and I was battle scarred, but alive.

And I had learned something else. People had studied insects. Some people had written about insects and thought they were important enough to put in the encyclopedia. Now I knew how to learn about who were the stingers and biters, and who could be rescued by hand. And I had learned that you can't just pry into someone else's world without upsetting things and maybe even causing a lot of pain for everyone involved.

My father wore a beekeeper hat and gloves and cleared out the nest from under the eaves. He did something to them first to quiet them. I suspect it was DDT and that they were permanently quieted, but at the time, he told me that when they were all asleep that he just moved them to a better home. It might be true. He never was much on killing things.

This thought leads me in two or, probably, more directions. Ah, the cluster method of producing ideas. My brain is a veritable mare's nest of thoughts, and they twist together like a Gordian Knot.

My father was not much on killing things. He didn't even swat flies but would catch them, then open the screen door and toss them outside, releasing them to fly back inside the very next time one of us came through the door. I recall that once when we were on the boat...and , as this was in my later childhood, we were on the Ohio River. We were moored so that we could eat our lunch far out on the water away from the bothersome flies on the land, but one busy, buzzing fly was on board with us. My mother was fruitlessly swatting at him and finally said to my father, "Eugene, swat that fly! It is driving me crazy to try and fix this lunch and keep that fly away from our food!"

And so my father caught the fly in one quick swipe of his nimble hand. Then he stood, looking a bit uncomfortable, thinking. He had no place to toss that fly. To toss him over the water just meant that he would rejoin us immediately as there was no way the fly would head out over the water toward land. We had no screen door to close that would protect our food and my mother from the outside world of our boat.

My mother looked at my father and said, "Just kill him."

My father winced. We were all locked in indecision. My brother and I wondered if our father would squish that big fly. My mother wondered if he would let it go to bother her again.

By this time I had an assortment of killing jars and little bottles because I had become an avid insect collector. I already had several flies in my collection, though, so I wasn't really wanting that fly, but I did think of a way to resolve the impasse between my mother and my father.

"How about we try to get that fly into one of my jars," I suggested. My father frowned, and I hurriedly added, "maybe not a killing jar. And then we can let him go when we get ashore," I finished, brightly.

It seemed like a reasonable solution and my father brightened a bit, too. The trouble started when we tried to get the little bugger out of my father's hand and into the jar. I got the jar and opened it. My father carefully moved his hand over the opening and tried to make certain that he could cover the top so the fly would go into the jar and not get free. He slowly opened his hand and the fly immediately got away and flew directly into my mother's hair. My brother, who had been following this with great curiosity, rolled up his comic book and swatted my mother's head, smearing the fly in her hair. She was both startled by the vigorous swat and repulsed by the amount of fly gut she now had stuck in her hair. The look on her face told it all, and I felt sorry for my brother who had done a worthy deed in bravely disposing of the incorrigible fly, but was being rewarded with a look of alarm and repulsion. We all understood, though. We were afloat on the Ohio River. There was no bathtub or shower. My mother was to be stuck with fly gutted hair that she wouldn't be able to wash for at least another day, unless she decided to try to wash it in the muddy Ohio.

My mother just turned her annoyed look toward my father. "Why didn't you just swat it to start with, or squish it after you made the mistake of catching it," she said.

My father just shrugged and daintily wiped his fly catching hand with a damp rag.

My brother wiped the fly guts off of his comic book on the railing of the boat.

"That was pretty good aim," I said to him. He gave me a lopsided grin.

There is a dark side to the story of my father and his gentle, caring relationship with flies. He had a guilty conscience. As a boy he had garnered attention from his classmates with his fly circus. He would make a little set of circus-like rings, "usually three, like the Big Top" he told me, and then he would set up pieces of cork for obstacle courses and such. And then he would catch flies. He assured me that some types of flies made better circus performers than others,…and he said he would (oh, I can hardly stand to write this!) tear off their wings so they couldn't fly away, and he would put them in his little circus rings, and then they would run around, and it looked like they were performing! He told me that he even stuck some of them on the ends of needles that were stuck in the corks, and they would look like they were dancing. And he would show all the boys and then they would call over the girls, and the girls would, at first, be wondrous…and then they would realize what was happening, and they would faint…at least, some of them would faint. He got into trouble for his circus, and the teacher and the principal and his parents…well, he was born in 1912, and even with enlightened parents like his own, I can imagine what happened. Even if there was no corporal punishment, I can guess that it was the most shaming of lectures. It is interesting how these events play out.

Am I going far afield? Perhaps. I am swimming, and swimming, and searching for Rapunzel. In the first part of that fairy tale, there is a mother and a father, too. In some versions the father so loves the mother that he ventures into a dangerous place, the witch's garden, to steal something for her...but then, when he is caught, he does not stand up to the witch and neither does the mother although the different versions of the story vary on just how much the mother knows about the situation. It makes it hard to understand just why the baby is given over to the witch with so little fight.

Once I saw my father, who didn't like to kill even a fly, goaded into shooting a squirrel.

My mother's older brother seemed a harsh man who was full of anger. My mother's family avoided him as much as they could. They invited him to family events, but would sigh with relief when he would decline. There had been a terrible split in the family, (and I had been a little child witness to that quarrel...another story...) but my mother had tried to keep a connection with this brother and his family, and we found ourselves visiting them on occasion, and there would be the happy lightness of family, thinly stretched over some deep, deep anger and pain which we all could feel was there, but we didn't address. And, of course, some of us, the young cousins, didn't know and, I think, never have known where the pain came from or why it was there, and we didn't dare ask about it. We just had to pretend we didn't notice.

At any rate, during one of these visits, precipitated by my mother, my father was caught in a spot. I remember feeling that we had driven for quite a long time that day. We had been admiring the autumn leaves and enjoying the fine weather all morning. We had had a picnic lunch. My mother had told my brother and me that, if we had time, and if the weather was right, and if we found ourselves close to where my uncle and his family lived, we would stop to see them. She had called them, and they knew we might stop by. My brother was not particularly excited about a visit to my uncle's farm, because there were no boys in the family, and he was not particularly interested in farms, farm animals, or farming at all. I, however, was excited. I loved the idea of a farm…growing things, animals, trees and the world of nature. And there were three girl cousins, even though the youngest cousin was my brother's age and was, therefore several years older than I was. We hadn't been to their farm that I could remember. I thought it was because they lived so far away from us.

We arrived at the farm just after our picnic lunch. My mother had planned it so that we would not be a bother to my uncle's wife. I was a little disappointed because my experience had already taught me that when you visit someone, and it is mealtime, you get to try out something different to eat and usually there is cake.

My uncle came out onto the porch of the old farmhouse as we drove up the lane. He was a big man to me, and he had on bib overalls and big heavy boot-like shoes. He could not have been more different from my father, who always dressed nattily and was so careful of his appearance that my mother called him "neat and sweet".

Slowly, from behind my uncle, I saw figures of my thin, worried looking aunt and, one by one, my three girl cousins as they materialized in his shadow. There was Juanita, who was my brother's age and was wiry and rangy looking, but with an open smile, and Barbara who was older and more serious looking…more like her mother, I thought. Last was Martha. She was a little heavier than her sisters and had on an apron and was still holding a dish that she must have been drying from doing up the lunch dishes.

We parked the car and slowly got out as the other family moved cautiously toward us, apparently unsure of how to welcome us. Finally my father smiled his way forward and offered a handshake to his brother-in-law and my mother hugged her sister-in-law and then gave her brother an awkward hug. My brother and I stood back, waiting for the cousins to be reintroduced to us. They had grown up since we had last seen them at a family funeral several years before. Juanita took the lead and suggested we come on inside to see her pet raccoon. I was in Heaven. Imagine a pet raccoon!

Juanita's mother and Martha both squealed. "You didn't bring that pest into the house again, did you?" Juanita's mother asked.

"No, mother, just up into the mud room."

Mudroom, whoever heard of a mudroom! Oh, this place is Paradise. So I thought.

Juanita showed my brother and me to a little built-on shed that was right outside the back kitchen door. All around the sides there were hooks from which hung jackets that smelled of animals, and, leaning against the walls under the jackets were boots that were caked with dried mud. I guessed that the name, 'mudroom' had come from those dirty boots. Off to one side was a small wooden box

36

with a piece of chicken wire weighted down with a large rock covering the top. A small hand was stretching thin black fingers up through the mesh.

"Here", said Juanita, "meet Racky, my raccoon. He is still a baby, but he is eating OK now, so we think he will live." She lifted the rock from the box, and we peered down into the raccoon's dark face as he, equally curious, peered up into our faces.

I was thrilled. I had never been so close to a baby raccoon. It was so much cuter than a human baby. It was cuter than a puppy or a kitten. I loved it! Juanita was the luckiest person in the world. A farm. Wild animal babies for pets.

Racky was feeling braver now, with the chicken wire off of his box. He nimbly hopped up to the edge of the box as Juanita made a grab for him. She held him firmly and carefully.

"Can I hold him?" I asked.

"I don't think you had better try it," Juanita said, shaking her head. "He bites, and he doesn't know that he will die if he gets away from us. He is too young to make it on his own, and his mother is dead. I'm afraid that if you accidently let go of him, well, he would get away and die."

Just then Martha opened the kitchen door. "Juanita, take that animal back out to the barn where it belongs! It doesn't even belong there! It belongs in the woods!" she said. "I don't know what you think you are going to do with it if it lives long enough to grow up!" And she closed the door again.

"OK," said Juanita. "Back you go," she said as she put Racky back in the box and covered the top with the wire. "I just thought you guys might like to see him," she added.

My brother and I let her know that we were glad that we got to see Racky and then we followed her as she carried the box back across the yard and into the dusty dark of the big barn behind the house. She put Racky into a larger cage filled with straw and carefully latched the latch. Then we all returned to the house.

The adults were visiting in the living room. Juanita's mother was showing my mother some of her needlework. Barbara and Martha were both in 4-H, and they had made outfits for the fair. They had gone upstairs to put them on to show their handiwork to my mother.

My uncle had taken a gun out of a case and was showing it to my father. My brother gravitated to them. I knew that my father had a gun. It was a small rifle which he used for target shooting once in a great while. I'm not even sure why he had a gun in the first place really. Guns were not big items in my family.

Juanita asked me if I wanted to go outside and go exploring. I was delighted. I thought Juanita must have been able to read my mind! Just as we went outside, I heard my uncle say to my father, "Let's take it outside, and you can try it." I was surprised to hear my father say, somewhat hesitantly, "Alright."

My brother said, "Maybe I could shoot it, too!" My heart skipped a beat. If my father let my brother shoot it, maybe he would let me shoot it! My hopes were dashed a moment later when my father said, "No, this is your uncle's new gun and it's only for adults."

Juanita looked at me and then my brother and then at my father. I had the feeling that she had used that new gun, but wasn't saying anything.

We all four went outside. The afternoon was fading, and I knew that we would be leaving soon. I wanted to see my father shoot that gun, and I knew that pretty soon he would say that we had to leave because he didn't want to drive in the dark.

My father said, "Let's set up some cans on the fence post over there."

"Naw," my uncle said. "Follow me." So we all followed my uncle as he led us back into the thick oak grove off to one side of the house.

"We'll get us a squirrel," my uncle said.

I was unsure what to think. On the one hand the idea of shooting a squirrel was like something an Indian or a pioneer might do. Shooting a squirrel for food for your family. But then, on the other hand, it was killing an animal like Racky.

The grove was quiet. A crow called from the barnyard and there was a fluttering of leaves when a sparrow or some other little bird moved from branch to branch, but otherwise it was quiet.

My uncle paused and stared hard up into the trees. "There," he said, as he pointed up into the branches.

My father peered up into the trees but shook his head. "I don't see anything. Let's just go back and shoot cans. It's going to get dark, and I want to be on the road before it gets too dark."

Just then there was a rustling and a scolding from the branches above us. We all saw the squirrel who was angry at our invasion of his domain.

"There it is," said my uncle as he handed my father the gun.

"No," said my father, "it's your new gun."

My uncle frowned, "But I want you to have the chance to shoot it."

My father slowly took the gun. My brother said, "Go ahead Dad. You are a real good shot!"

My father straightened up, took aim, fired, and instantly, before the sound of the gun stopped reverberating through the quiet trees, the squirrel fell from the branch.

I was proud of my father, but I was sickened, too. My feelings were confused. My brother ran with my cousin to find the dead squirrel.

Juanita offered to skin the squirrel so we could have the hide. My brother said that he thought that there were people in boy scouts who knew how to tan a hide and maybe they would teach him if he had a hide to tan. We ended up with the squirrel skin nailed onto a board, ready for tanning, I guess. We all got into the car and left the farm and our mother's relatives. None of us said much.

I heard my mother ask about the dead squirrel that we were taking back with us, and I heard my father say that he had thought for a moment about purposely missing his mark, but, somehow, his pride in his marksmanship got in the way, and he thought that my brother and I might have been embarrassed if he missed. He had the feeling that my uncle didn't expect him to hit the squirrel, either.

My mother murmured something and just patted him on the leg.

I said, "Well, now we know that if we were Indians, we never would go hungry!"

No one else said anything more. That squirrel skin sat in our old stone basement on a ledge for as long as I lived in that house. As far as I know, no one ever learned how to tan a hide in our family.

******

Swimming. For some reason when I swim, in my mind, I can return to places where I have been, and to experiences I have had and then wondered about, and then the intense feelings come back and, sometimes, I can see things more clearly. Sometimes I can see that there might be another way of looking at an incident. It might be that there is something that a child, like the child Rapunzel, or Snow White, or Cinderella, has missed. A "backstory" of sorts. Did Rapunzel ever wonder about her parents? Did she know about the rampion? And Snow White…did she understand the painful jealousy and insecurity that drove her stepmother? Did Cinderella know that she was despised because of her father's failure to reassure her stepmother and stepsisters…or whatever was behind it all…perhaps a cultural system that pushes females into desperation because of their culturally required dependence upon men. Why do we need to reconcile with the members of our families before they die? Why is it such an important piece of advice? I think it is important to hear the older story, the story of the generation before because once they are gone it is even harder to discover the "backstory" that has shaped our life experiences. And I am swimming in backstory.

My mother's story is murky. I have only bits and pieces, and those are the bits and pieces she dropped like crumbs for me to follow…and many bits have been nibbled away in my memory over the years until I am no longer certain of their truth.

My mother was born into a family with four older children. The older children, at the time of her birth, already had memories of living in a shack-like structure on a homestead in New Mexico. The arid region was poor land for a farmer from Ohio, and my grandfather spent much of his time working as a dispatcher for the railroad. He had a good ear and was quick with the telegraph key…a skill that, with the arrival of the telephone, was soon outdated.

My grandmother was homesick. Life in New Mexico was lonely for her. She saw no one near her except the children and occasional Indians who stopped by to beg for hand-outs, and she watched the tumbleweeds blow first, in the morning, across from the east and then, in the evening, blow back again from the west. She waited for a chance to visit her neighbors, her husband's sister and family, but with no horse and buggy and four small children, visits were few and far between. When it rained, the rain came through the rickety, make-shift roof. My grandmother was exhausted and depressed.

My mother's oldest sister, the very reason for my grandparent's rather hurried-up marriage, told my mother that she remembered waking up one night in that shack during a violent downpour to see their mother hurrying around to place pans and bowls to catch the rain water as it dripped through the leaky roof. My aunt saw her mother's look of dismay as she tried to creep back into her bed and realized that there, directly above her, was a leak right over her pillow. My grandmother looked up at the increasingly steady stream, and then she simply reached for her umbrella, opened it, propped it over her head, and then fell back into an exhausted sleep.

I have such a vivid image in my mind of my grandmother protecting her sleep from the intrusive rain...but where was my grandfather? Was he sleeping through this? Was he in town at the railway station listening for the tap of the telegraph? Was he worried about his little family, alone in the storm, on the open prairie? What must it have been like to wake up every day with children to feed, and wash, and clothe, and food to put up for winter, and hungry strangers stopping by who would see you as hopelessly vulnerable. Nothing bad happened as far as I know, and so it would seem that the strangers, who were always referred to as Indians, were certainly not ones to take advantage of a small thin, homesick woman with little children, alone on the arid prairie...

I never knew my grandmother, my mother's mother, well. By the time I was born she was an old woman who sat in a rocking chair and smiled an odd, somewhat frightening, smile. My mother had Olan Mills take a photo of my grandmother and me when I was about three months old, and I have it still. She is sitting and holding me. To my mother's great dismay, I blew a bubble just as the photographer finally got my grandmother to smile for him. She often told me that she was so disappointed that I had done that and ruined the picture. I look at the picture and see a rather contented looking little baby with a damp chin and an almost crazed looking old woman holding the child. My grandmother is trying to show pleasure, but her face is twisted somehow. Now I think that she might have been suffering from Parkinson's disease, a disease that seems to affect the muscles of the face. But no one has ever suggested that to me. It is only my own thought.

Once, when I was very little, my mother and brother and I were visiting my mother's oldest sister. Oh, I have since learned that there was much more to this story, too. It was my mother's first long trip driving our family car to visit her family. When we arrived, my oldest male cousin, who was actually closer to my parents age than to my age, jumped in his car and went to visit my father…to keep him company while his wife and children were gone…and they had quite a little adventure which ended with my cousin asleep in the bathroom with his right hand in the toilet bowl..but then, that is another story…

Anyway, at my Aunt and Uncle's house, my brother was playing with our younger boy cousin, but I was afraid of that cousin. He was an aggressive, sassy boy who was several years older than my brother and so seemed quite old to me. I didn't know much about him, and I was just as glad to be a little girl and therefore be unimportant to him because he seemed to have something bothering him. He seemed to want to show my brother that he was stronger and meaner than anyone else…and he succeeded, because when all the other adults were out of the room except my silent, grimacing grandmother in her rocking chair, he glanced around the room, smiled a mean teeth smile at me and then walked over to my grandmother and kicked her hard in the shin. He had on the heavy leather boots that farm boys wore back then. Her usually rather passive face contorted with pain, and she bent forward to hold her leg, and he danced away, looking at me, challenging me to do something. My grandmother had made no more sound than a soft moan. I watched my cousin until he left the room and then I ran to tell my mother, but I felt I couldn't just blurt out this terrible thing in front of my cousin's mother. Who would believe that a big boy like my cousin would do such a terrible, cruel thing to a helpless old woman?

After I had whispered my tattle to my mother, she ran to my grandmother, and my aunt followed, asking what was wrong. My mother told her sister what I had said, and, much to my surprise, my aunt didn't deny that it could have happened. She just shook her head sorrowfully and knelt down with my mother to look at my grandmother's leg.

I have no idea what might have happened to my cousin. I don't know if he was accused, and he denied it, or if he admitted to doing it, or if the whole episode was ignored. I know that my grandmother came to stay with us for a while, and then that she left our house to stay with a different daughter…and that the ceiling fell in our little living room where my grandmother had slept only a few days before, and my mother wept and said she was so glad that that hadn't happened while her mother had been with us.

My cousin grew older, of course. I remember seeing him at a family picnic with a girlfriend whom he later married. I assumed that he had outgrown his meanness, and my mother urged me to forget what I had seen. I remember smiling and exchanging a few awkward sentences with his girlfriend. She wasn't much older than I was really, about my brother's age. I couldn't help wondering if my cousin were nice to her or if he kicked her in the shins. I felt badly that I wasn't forgetting, that I was holding a grudge and not giving him "the benefit of a doubt".

Not long after I met his girlfriend, my mother told me that they had married and then they had a baby son, and then my cousin was killed in a motorcycle accident. It was said that he was showing off at an intersection, or something…trying to impress some girls who were watching him, it was whispered. Surely not, I thought, with a young wife and tiny baby son at home. But maybe he was just kicking her in the shins. Forgive me, mother. I can't forget that mean teeth smile, and I don't know his 'backstory' and there is no one I can ask.

I need to go a different direction. There are so many mean teeth stories in my life and the 'backstory' keeps going back and sometimes comes to a dead end (no pun intended). I know that my mother and father and grandparents and great-grandparents are telling me to forgive and forget and yet they are begging me to understand and put the pieces together, and I can't do that without the 'backstory'. So many mixed messages. Oh, Rapunzel, what a tangled story!

Did Rapunzel notice insects? Surely she saw butterflies. Everyone sees butterflies. But did she notice beetles? There are many more beetles than butterflies. And I would imagine that she would have encountered flies and mosquitoes! Wait, not everyone knows mosquitoes! I assumed that they lived in every climate because I have heard of an African story called "Why the mosquito buzzes in your ear" or something similar to that. And we all have heard of the death and destruction caused by mosquitoes in the various South

American, African, Central American, and Southern US areas…but I am not sure about Europe or Fairy. Perhaps there are no mosquitoes there…

Once, when my granddaughter was about four years old, I was visiting my daughter, her mother, and her family in San Diego. I could not believe the weather in February in Southern California, having driven from Minnesota in ice and snow all the way to Kansas City on that long stretch of Interstate 29 that goes by Sioux Falls and Omaha and St. Joe. I had left my car in KC with friends so that I could take advantage of frequent flyer miles in order to travel to this sunny Mecca, and I was somewhat in shock at the difference. My granddaughter had a swing fastened in such a way that when she went up and up she could see far over the highway and across to the mountains and over the red roofs of all of the neighbors who lived below her. And she wanted me to push her in her swing. "Grandmama Bear," she asked, "How high am I?" And I answered, "Oh, you are flying as high as an eagle!" And she laughed and said, "An eagle!" Then she asked again, "Grandmama, how high am I now?" And so I said, "You are as high as an airplane!" And she laughed and asked again, "Oh, Grandmama, how high am I now?" And I said, "Now you are flying as high as a mosquito" and my mind was racing to think of all the other flying things I could think of as I could see how this game was going to go, when she said, "a moss-ki-toe. But Grandmama, what IS a moss –ki-toe?" and she put her feet down, dragging herself to a stop from her high-flying adventure.

A child who had never encountered a mosquito! And, probably had never swatted, too late, at a no-see-um, or endured the tell-tale drip of blood behind her ear that is left from the bite of the ever malicious black fly!

I confronted my daughter with this information. Just how high of a tower had she constructed for my granddaughter, that the child had no knowledge of these things?

"Ah," my daughter laughed. "One of the best things about living in San Diego…no moss-ki-toes!"

I sent so many stickers and stampers and coloring books and such to my far-away granddaughters in San Diego. I had no idea that one of them was terrified of spiders and insects and creepy-crawlers!! Imagine having a long distance grandmamma who sends you all sorts of things covered with the very things that give you the "willys". I was the witch grandmama –probably imagined to be covered with warts and odd hairs and crazed eyes.

Oh grandmothers with crazed eyes! My mother was born after the family had pulled up stakes in New Mexico. The family had left in failure. The new telephones had made my grandfather obsolete and unneeded by the railroad, and the Pasamoto in New Mexico had defeated his efforts to farm, and he hadn't obtained enough land to be successful as a rancher, either. They had returned to live closer to his wife's family. She wasn't well, and it seemed to be more than homesickness. My grandfather's family did not seem to welcome him back. He had sold his inheritance to his brothers in order to strike out for New Mexico. Now he could work for his brothers on what would have been his own land had his girlfriend not become pregnant and had her brothers and family not forced a marriage. It wasn't that he didn't love her. At least my mother thought that there was love, or what she called 'love' between them. But there was something else, and I can't help but think it was resentment, and a sense of mutual blame, and I sense that my grandmother carried a heavier burden than she could bear, not only for what she must have felt was her own poor judgment, but also for her husband's poor judgment.

The night that my mother was born, my grandmother disappeared. The midwives were two of my grandfather's sisters. And as they held the newborn, somehow, my grandmother managed to make her escape from the old, rented farmhouse. She was wearing nothing but her nightgown, and she ran, barefooted, across the harvested fields and into a grove of trees. She was going to get away from everything at last. She was searching for rampion that her husband had forgotten to get for her. But it was November and the rampion was withered and dried and plowed under the ground into a grave. It was All Souls Day. It was the Day of the Dead.

The sisters, wringing their hands with worry, greeted my grandfather with the news of my grandmother's disappearance when he returned from his brother's fields and barns. He left to look for her without taking even a glance at his newborn daughter. His older children stood silently in the shadows feeling his wrath and fury and frustration as he passed them on his way out to search for her who was needed to nurse this child and feed and care for the others. He could barely make out her footprint in the hardening, plowed earth, but he could see the grove of trees, and he knew how she had pined for trees when in New Mexico. He knew where she was headed. He found her by the light of his lantern. She was collapsed and cold to the touch, but was not quite dead. It was that Day, though. It really was the Day of the Dead. In the northern night the stars gleamed in the cold air and the skeletons danced just as they had in New Mexico. He carried her home, stumbling his weary way back across the fields, and his fretting sisters tucked her cold, motionless body next to her warm, whimpering baby. She survived death in some ways. She became silent, though, as if her spirit would leave her if she spoke. She barely whispered. Nevertheless, she did bear one more child. My mother's younger brother was born barely two years after my mother.

I am painting a very dark picture of my grandfather, my mother's father. Perhaps I am not being fair. My mother adored him. She seemed to understand something about him, or maybe she felt that life had simply not been fair to him. There is more there, I know.

I have a photo of one of my San Diego granddaughters sitting next to a skeleton on a bench in Mexico. She is about four years old with just a cap of white-blonde hair and a giddy smile on her face as she holds hands with the skeleton. It is the Day of the Dead and my blonde, fair-skinned granddaughter is with her family, visiting her father's grandmother who lives in a comfortable ocean-side home in Baja. My little granddaughter has come to terms with the skeletons, and she is comfortable with them. My daughter tells me that she was surprised that her younger daughter loved the skeletons so much, because her older girl was more hesitant and was a little afraid of all the gaiety surrounding the emblems of death. I am glad that I have a granddaughter who is brave enough to hold the skeleton's hand. I will try to be as brave.

A friend of mine developed breast cancer and through the folly of denial and the fear of pushing her family into poverty because of medical bills, she waited too long for a diagnosis and only lived a year after she finally saw the doctor. I was angry with her, and myself, because she had told me of the lump she had found much earlier...in the summer, and she had responded to my alarm by assuring me that she was to see a doctor soon, even though she thought that medical bills would bankrupt her family. And I had believed her. We were swimming buddies, and we swam together in a spring-fed pond. Usually she and I were the only ones in the coldest part of that water-weed filled, reed choked pond, because others seemed afraid of the possibility of snakes among the weeds. My friend was a racer, but she tolerated my slower, easy-going pace. Sometimes she swam loops around me, taunting me good-naturedly, trying to get me to accept her challenge to race. But I knew better than to accept. I am no racer. I just love the water. She and I swam among the reeds and laughed at the frogs we frightened, and we chased the whirligig beetles ahead of us. The summer ended, and we didn't see each other at the pond. I didn't check up on her right away, because I was busy with my own life, and all the things that must be done before the winter sets in and strands northern folk in their homes, and I thought that she would have called me if she had a problem…if she needed a babysitter while she had chemo or something…I didn't know much about cancer at the time.

When I learned that she had put off her appointment, for months, and that finally she had gone in and found that there was nothing much to be done for her, I was stunned. I went to see her, but found the whole family in such pain, I could hardly bear it. We snatched a moment alone, away from her husband and children, and I have never felt so helpless. I could only listen and nod. When she went to the hospital to die, I was one of several people who took turns sitting with her, waiting. I talked to her about our swimming times. I listened to her whispered comments. I held her hand. Finally, the nurses brought her young, preteen daughter in to see her. My friend was barely conscious because of the medications and painkillers, but she managed a weak smile for her daughter, who had quickly pressed herself against the wall as far away from her mother's death as she could get. We three were alone in the room. Finally I reached my hand to my friend's daughter and grabbed her frightened hand. I was, at first, stretched between them…holding my friend's hand with my right hand and holding her daughter's hand with my left hand. I didn't say anything. What is there to say? As her daughter began to conquer her fear, she slowly moved closer to me. I am not certain just how long it took, but finally, we were close to each other and after a while I was able to move her hand into her mother's hand, and I was able to stand up and kiss my friend goodbye and leave her with her daughter.

I must move on in this search for 'backstory'. Away from this pain.

******

My mother told a story about some of the happiest, most carefree moments of her childhood. Down the road from the house where she spent her youngest years there lived an elderly widow who had a lovely little garden, and in the garden there was a swing…the kind with benches on either side where one could sit with a dear friend and rock back and forth together and admire the yard and garden. My mother and her younger brother would skip down the road and ask this lady if they could sit in her swing, and she would always say yes to them. They would go into the garden and climb into the swing, and my mother and her brother would swing and sing every song they knew over and over. The lady would watch them, and sometimes she would give cookies and lemonade to them, especially if she thought they must be thirsty after all that singing!

Years later, after my grandparents had died and both my brother and I had moved away from our home, my father bought a garden swing like the one my mother remembered, and he put it up in the big garden in back of the house. My mother enjoyed swinging in it. And it pleased her when her grandchildren and the neighbor children played on her "Grandma swing!"

I don't remember that my mother would swim very much. She would put on a bathing suit and sit in the sun, but she was terribly self-conscious of her body, which had changed after childbirth from being thin and stylish to being, in her words, 'dumpy'. She was just over 5 feet tall and so she would preface that description with "short" and say "I have a short and dumpy figure now." I didn't see her that way, and I didn't understand why it bothered her so much, and I wished that she would just put on her bathing suit and swim and stop worrying about how she looked.

But no one had ever looked at me, so I didn't understand what it might have meant to "lose your looks".

I was very thin, even as a baby. As a child I had 'chicken legs'. I'm not sure what that meant but when I see pictures of myself, I see a child with legs that are the same distance around from thigh to calf with even thinner ankles. And I see a child with long thin arms. And a waif-like face. I entered puberty rather late and didn't fill out anywhere until even later. The long and short of this is…I would put on any bathing suit I could find, and I jumped into the water whenever I could.

My father would wear his bathing suit and an undershirt, and he would get into the water to work on the boat or to ski or do what we called "surf boarding", which was accomplished by riding on a large, heavy, specially shaped board which was tied by a rope to a boat and then was pulled behind the fast moving boat while the 'surfer' stood and held onto reins that were fastened to the board. I think it might have been rather dangerous, but, at that time, I never thought of that and I started surfing that way almost as soon as I could stand up. There are even photos of me sitting between my father's legs as he and I surfboarded together! But he rarely just went swimming.

Water! Some of my best memories are of riding on the prow of our boat, especially the small cruiser which was the last of a long line of boats we had. My father would criss-cross the wakes of other boats to try to splash me with water as I sat with my legs dangling over the prow. Now it seems so reckless! And sometimes I did get thrown off! But it was into the water, and I loved the water!

Once, when I was a bit older, I was sitting on the bow, legs hanging over, straddling the prow light, when the Delta Queen came around the bend of the river. Seeing the Queen was always a thrill and everyone on the river would make way for her, and then we would honk our horns and blow our whistles and ring our bells and wave to the lucky people who were traveling aboard the Queen! This time in particular, was exciting because she started to play calliope music for us in response to our attention. After she passed by, my father started to criss-cross her wake because she made such huge waves, and he knew I loved to pretend that they were ocean waves. Unfortunately, I had stood up to greet the Queen, and I hadn't gotten reseated completely before he hit the first wave. Off I went, right into those gigantic, to me at least, waves. My mother screamed, apparently, but I didn't really hear because at first I went right under the water. Then, of course, I popped up and paddled around in the pitch of the waves. I tossed my head a bit to clear my sight and when I could see, I saw my father wheeling the boat around to get me. I waved to my parents, and my mother told me later that she was terrified until she saw that not only had I not lost my glasses, but that I was laughing! She scolded my father, anyway, but it became a memory he and I shared. A happy memory, although, I suppose it could have been disastrous.

It is often that way with memories. Some of the best ones have a possible dark side. Are they the best because they could have been bad? It reminds me of the Lincoln Steffens story, "The Miserable, Merry Christmas". The child, young Lincoln Steffens, I think, believes that because he has said he wants nothing if he can't have a horse for Christmas, that he is getting nothing. Indeed he seems to be getting nothing, because the man whom the father hired to bring a pony on Christmas morning has gotten lost and is quite late…and the father, determined to have his gift be a surprise, lets the boy suffer until the pony is delivered…and the father asks the boy, later in life, if that was the best or the worst Christmas ever…The point Lincoln Steffens makes, I think, is that sometimes we don't really know what is best or worst. Sometimes we never know. And I do think that some of the moments I think of as best are best because they could have been so "worst".

Rapunzel is supposed to have had beautiful hair. Strong hair. I had hair that was neither beautiful nor strong. If hair is the important motif in 'Rapunzel' then why was I drawn to it even if I was drawn to hate it? Could it be that I so hated my own hair that I longed for long, thick hair like she was supposed to have had? No. I don't think so.

My mother was interested in my hair, but I couldn't have cared less. I had straw for hair, and I was OK with that except when for a time when I was a teenager and the girls in my class tried to force my hair to do something conformist. At that time I gave a half hearted attempt to fluff and tease and make my unruly, limp, fine hair do something. I hated the feel of hairspray. I hated curlers. But most of all I hated the waste of time that accompanies messing with your hair. I wanted to be reading, or prowling around looking for insects, or figuring out what stars belonged in what constellation. Staring at my hair using hand mirrors to see the back and the sides, and then trying to coax it into some rigid shape that resembled the hairdo on a girl in a magazine…a girl who probably had thick, fat hair that liked to sit on the girl's head in contorted ways, ugh! And, besides the time it would have taken! It really is very hard to have a bouffant hairdo and swim. I think that is what the other girls called it, a 'bouffant'.

The other girls only tried to do something with my hair once that I remember. It was boring, and I felt my patience tried as they played hairdresser with my head. I remember after what seemed like hours of hot rollers and hairspray and endless teasing, that my hair still looked rather sad. I pushed it up a bit. It was like a sticky, rigid mass of spider web, barely concealing all that teasing underneath, and my one gesture caused the one girl who was still struggling with it and hadn't given up, to say, "That helped! It looks better now, don't you think so?" I think it did look better, but there was no way that I was going to spend time like that trying to make my hair into a space helmet for my head.

So I don't think that I was overly conscious of Rapunzel's hair. There was something else in that story that triggered my aversion and obsession. Something else that etched itself into my unconscious.

******

I have mentioned my passion for studying and collecting insects, but I haven't written much about it. I usually kept a pill bottle with me to contain any different insect I encountered. I especially did this after one unfortunate experience I had at camp. Every year after I reached a certain age, I went to camp. I loved going to camp, because at camp, I could be a completely different person. No one there knew me or knew what the people in my hometown thought about me. No one knew that I lived in that house with the hidden garden and a 'guesthouse'. I was just the blonde, skinny girl in cabin 5.

Anyway, most years I went to church camp (which was coed), Girl Scout camp (which was not coed), and 4-H camp. Five or six weeks of my summer were spent at various camps…and then I usually spent several weeks with my relatives in Colorado. These experiences broadened my world, as well as gave my parents and grandparents some respite from me. I, of course, thought that they missed me, but in rethinking it all, I suspect that they enjoyed the break. Sometimes my brother went to camps, too, but usually he stayed home and had 'quality time' with my family. He was enough older than I, that by the time I went off to camp, he was a genuine help to my family in the business that my father and grandfather continued to operate.

But back to camp and insects. Because of my interest in entomology, I collected different insects from wherever I was. Once at camp, I learned the hard way that 'red' can signify danger.

As all of us were walking down a trail, on a hike I guess, I spotted a bright red insect scurrying along the ground. I stopped, of course, and, of course, the children behind me began to run into each other and then they started to push their way around me, looking to see if I were tying my shoe, or what. In the commotion the red insect began to scurry in a confused way in the leaf litter, and I was in hot pursuit. Without a bit of caution, caught up in the chaos and driven to catch that insect and then get up and move along, as the hike leader was now calling back to see 'whatever was the matter', I grabbed the insect, and it stung me.

The sting was so hard that I gasped. It was very painful. I dropped the insect and watched it through teary eyes as it scampered away. My whole arm felt numb with the pain. The hike leader had gotten to me by that time and in the excitement, he somehow got the idea that I had been attacked by this vicious wasp type of insect and that that was why the line of children had stopped...I had been attacked, and then, I had stopped and fallen to the ground and nearly been trampled by the children who had been behind me. That is what he thought.

I wasn't saying anything. I was in pain. As the story developed around me, I liked it better than the truth. It seemed a better story than the truth. After all, the whole incident and all the kerfuffle that followed had been my fault. I had been the aggressor. The insect was merely defending itself, and I had stupidly picked it up with my bare hands. I knew ants could bite and it had walked like an ant walks. I even knew what kind of ant it was because I had seen it in my insect identification book. It was a 'velvet ant', sometimes called a 'cow killer'. I was beginning to understand just how it had gotten that nickname.

The counselor wanted to know what kind of insect had stung me and when I said it was an ant, he was confounded. No ants that he knew of could bite hard enough to make someone fall down. Now it began to dawn on him that I might have some sort of allergy and that maybe we had all better head back to the campground so I could get to a doctor. The groans from the other children warned me to try to stop this nonsense, but I was at a loss. My arm really hurt and I wondered if maybe I might be similar enough to a cow to be killed by that little red beast.

I mustered up my courage and went ahead to say to the counselor that I thought that my 'attacker' was a type of wasp-ant. This didn't seem to help the situation, because he just kept turning the whole group around to head back down the trail. He walked with me as I stumbled along, feeling miserable with pain and regret.

The clincher for this episode came during my interview with the doctor. He ferreted the truth out of me. It seems that he was an amateur entomologist himself. He warned me to avoid catching strange insects with my bare hands. I had already figured that out! And he suggested, more kindly, that I carry pill bottles around with me at all times...and he gave me one to start me off. As far as I know, he never told anyone that I had precipitated the attack. The pain in my arm soon dissipated, and I rejoined my group of campers.

Because of this painful episode I began to appreciate the advice to never pick up strange insects, and I did try to keep a pill bottle with me just in case I spotted an interesting specimen. However, when you go swimming at camp, you wear a bathing suit and carry a towel. There isn't really a place to put a pill bottle, and my next experience happened when I had gone swimming.

Our swimming times were broken up with lessons in swimming and free time swimming. The various swimming class levels alternated lessons so the swimming area would not be so crowded. I was always in the advanced class and, therefore, in the deepest part of the swimming area. Usually there weren't many of us in the advanced group, and we would have the diving platform and the deep water all to ourselves, but, on occasion, the teachers would have the intermediate class swim out to the platform, and at that time, we deep-water people would have to get out of the way. The swimming instructors would blow the whistle and move us up onto the beach to wait, rest, play in the sand, and go to the bathroom.

During one of these rest times, I went to the bathroom and on my way into the building I spotted a huge, black beetle that had obviously flown against the building in its blundering awkward flight. I wanted it for my collection! I looked around frantically for a container to use, but I couldn't find anything. I looked down into the trash can that stood by the bathroom door. Nothing that I could use. I rushed into the bathroom and cast my eyes about, …nothing, nothing, and then I saw it! Up on the ledge between the roof and the building, resting in the hole of a concrete block was a small metal box. I reached up and pulled it out. It was an old tin box of the type in which breath mints sometimes were sold. I opened it up and inside of it there were a few pills of some type. I could tell that they weren't breath mints, but I didn't know what they were. Anyway I took them out of the box and put the pills back into the concrete hole. Then I rushed outside and went looking for the beetle. As I found it and scooped it into the box and closed it, a girl came up to me. "What are you doing with my box!" she said.

"Your box!" I exclaimed. "I found this box!"

"It's mine," she cried out. "Give it to me!"

"No," I cried as vehemently as I could, while clutching the box, with its lively treasure trapped safely inside, close to my chest. She gave me an angry shove and ran off toward the beach. I watched as she ran to one of the lady counselors and got her attention. She pointed to me, and then I saw them coming up the walk toward me. I had a bad feeling.

The counselor didn't waste many words. She asked me where I had found the box, and I told her. She asked me if I had looked inside. And I told her that I had. She asked me what I had seen inside the box, and I said that I had seen some funny looking pills. She asked me if I had taken them and eaten them. I said no. She asked me to give her the box so I, very reluctantly, did.

As she held the box, she explained to me that the girl who had challenged me had a serious allergy to bees and that the pills were there in case she was stung while she was at the beach. I was aghast. I knew that that could be very dangerous. I had heard of it before. As I stood there, shocked, the counselor opened the box.

My beetle put its front feet up on the edge of the box, opened its black top wings and flew into the air, right by the counselor's stunned face. She dropped the box and staggered backwards. The girl started shrieking, hysterically. Another counselor came running up from the beach. I was watching that beetle fly. It was whirring rather loudly, and it whacked into the roof of the bathroom before heading awkwardly off toward the woods.

The second counselor was quieting the girl. The first counselor regained her composure and turned to me, white with fury and asked, "Where are the pills!"

"I put them back in the hole. They are fine. We can put them back in the box. I didn't know they were important. I just thought…" I couldn't think what I had thought. What had I thought?

The girl started shrieking again. "Don't put my pills back in that dirty old box that had that dirty old bug in it!" she howled.

"Bugs aren't dirty," I retorted indignantly. "And it was a beetle, not a bug!"

The first counselor had had enough of me. She grabbed my arm and dragged me into the bathroom and made me show her where the pills were. She checked with the girl that they were, indeed, the correct pills.

The swimming teacher blew a whistle, which was to let everyone know that it was time to switch back to our regular swimming places. I hesitated, but the counselor indicated that I should go back down. As I left the bathroom I heard the counselor suggest that the girl take the pills back to her cabin, and the girl answered, "No! She touched them and she probably touched that bug!"

I almost stopped to tell her that 'not touching' had been the whole point...but I thought better of it.

******

Not touching. Oh, Rapunzel and I have something in common there! To be in a tower with only an old, cranky witch...well, that doesn't sound like a very cuddly childhood. And I had a rather un-cuddly childhood myself!

To begin with, I had that 'eczema' when I came home from the hospital with my mother. That doesn't invite much cuddling. My mother said that she would try to hold me, but I would scream as though in pain. The doctor tried all sorts of treatments, but I was an oozy mess. Not very appealing. Finally, they decided to change my formula. My mother hadn't even tried to breastfeed me. I was born at that moment in time when breastfeeding was considered unladylike and plebian…a little lower class. And so I was formula fed, and I think it didn't agree with me. My mother thought that I had picked up the eczema from her, because she had read magazines that the nurses had given her from the waiting room and, perhaps, had not washed her hands carefully enough before holding me. However, I suspect that it was the formula, because after trial and error with all sorts of formulas and recipes, my father located a woman (old and cranky perhaps?) who had a nanny goat and …I thrived on goat's milk. I recovered from the eczema, but the pattern seemed set. I was a wiry, restless baby, for the most part, and used adults to get a better vantage point of the world. I don't remember any of this, of course, but I do think I was a bit off about being held. I have memories about squirming free from various constricting adults.

My parents weren't very cuddly either. My mother had had that rough beginning with her mother, but, I think she was probably cuddled by her siblings. I found, among her things after she died, a little colored glass cup with a note in it. The note said, "I won this for being the "prettiest baby" at the county fair. My sisters had entered me in the contest and then had tirelessly rounded up votes for me from everyone they could persuade to do so who visited the fairgrounds!"

I suspect those three older sisters enjoyed dressing and playing with their little sister. They may have felt responsible for her, and, perhaps, a little sorry for her, too, since their mother was so ill all the time my mother was a baby. And then along came a second baby! Those girls may have felt that my mother, truly, was their very own baby to care for!

My father's cuddle story is stranger. He was surrounded by female figures. Both of his grandmothers lived with the family, and he had two older sisters. All five children were born within eight or nine years, so they were all pretty young. One would think that there would have been a good deal of cuddling going on in that house! But my father did not like to be touched. When anyone tried to touch him, he would laugh and pull away and tell, again and again, the story that he had been told about himself as a child. "If someone tried to pick me up, I would pull away and put my arms out and say, 'No, no, mine body!!'" He used the first person familiar because that was the way his grandmothers spoke!

So I wasn't reared in a very cuddly home. I don't know if it was different for my brother. If it was then, perhaps the eczema was the culprit…or my own irascible personality. I do know that being around a standoffish father paid off for me when, as an adult, I was cast as Chelsea in a touring theater production of "On Golden Pond". In one scene I was to try to give my distant and cool 'father' a hug, and he was to rebuff me. Every time I tried to hug my stage 'father', he would, simply, hug me back. The director would yell and stamp his feet, but my stage 'father' seemed to have no idea how to rebuff a hug.

Finally, I thought about it and said to him, "Look, do what my father does, when I try to hug him. Put up your arms and try to pretend you are having a hard time seeing what time it is on your watch. You know…you can't quite get it to line up with your bifocals!"

My stage father was amazed and a little dubious, but from then on, we did it that way and it was perfect. We could hear whispers from the audience at that very quiet moment as people realized that my 'Dad' was still not able to hug me back!"

I never told my father about that. I doubt that he realized that he did this…I don't think he was aware that his insistence on protecting himself, "mine body", was a rebuff to those who loved him.

My father always insisted that he couldn't hold a baby, that babies were too fragile. I had grown up with that notion, but I didn't accept it. I had seen other men hold babies…not men of my father's era, or of my grandfather's era, but men of my age. They held babies all the time and many of the men I knew were proud of their baby care skills! It wasn't that babies were too fragile for men to hold, obviously. I wanted my father to hold my children. I hoped that he would discover that touch was not so bad. At first I wasn't very successful. It wasn't that he didn't like my children. He just seemed to be frightened of holding them. When my son was born, my father and mother came to visit us in our little apartment. My husband was gone and I tried to hand my son to my father so that my mother and I could do some particular task, but he declined. Finally I spread a blanket on the floor and put my baby down on it. Then, as I left the room, I told my father to call to me if there was a problem. My mother and I were busy for quite a while and when I looked in on my father and my son, I found my father lying on the floor on his stomach. My tiny son was also lying on his stomach. My son's head was bobbing around as he unsteadily tried to hold it up in order to peer right into my father's eyes. I had never imagined my father getting right down on the floor to look my son in the eye, but he did.

It took my father a long time and many grandchildren to overcome his fear of holding babies, but he did it. We have a snapshot of my father, robed in a hospital gown, sitting in a chair in the hospital, holding my youngest child minutes after she was born. My father had come a long way.

Snapshots. I came across an old family photo of a gathering at my mother's grandparents' home which included my mother's father and all of his siblings. On the back was a separate piece of paper carefully glued in place, and written on it, in tiny, faded writing, were the names of almost everyone in the snapshot. I read them over carefully because I was interested in seeing those sisters of my grandfather who had accidently let my grandmother escape out into the night. I found them, sitting close together among their brothers and holding their youngest sister.,.but there was another boy a little off to the side. He was younger yet, and had rather large ears and seemed to be unhappy about sitting for this photo. I wondered who he might be. I carefully went over the names again, and then again as it seemed that his name wasn't there. The writing was faded, but it didn't look as though anything had been rubbed off. Who was the mystery boy? I was dismayed because I had no one whom I could ask. The picture was so old that everyone who would have known had already died. I felt oddly sad to have a photo of my own family and not know if this was a neighbor who had just dropped by, or if this was a younger brother of my grandfather whose name hadn't been listed on the back for some reason.

A few days went by and I forgot all about him. As I cleared some things off my desk one day, my daughter came in and picked up the picture. "Who are these people?" she asked and then she turned the photo over and deftly removed the glued on piece of paper.

"Oh, don't lose that!" I cried out. "That little paper has the names of all those people and they are your ancestors! If we lose that paper I won't know who is who!"

My daughter looked perplexed. As she peered down on the faded, little slip of paper, I saw, written on the back, the missing name. His name was Walter, and he was the baby of the family. My baby had found him!

******

I need for someone to have left another slip of paper with something written on it to answer my questions. I need a snapshot. I need to find this out.

I'm guessing that Rapunzel loved birds. When I swim, I sometimes float on my back and watch the birds circling in the sky far above me. I used to think that I would like to fly like a bird, but now I am content to move across the water and on land. Now I have a fear of falling, and falling out of the sky would be a very bad feeling, I think. I can not tell the birds apart when they are so far above me. They fade into the sky. I've noticed that some of them fly in distinctive ways that I can recognize, but most of them seem to be headed for someplace I can't see and their shapes and movements are not so different from one another that I can say with certainty that this one is a hawk and this one is a crow. As I float on my back, I vow to dig out my bird books with silhouettes of flying birds and, at least, try to learn how to tell them apart.

I'm guessing that Rapunzel thought about flying away from her tower. Right out of that window and into the sky. But what a big sky!

So many of the birds that I have watched have simply darted from branch to branch, or from the ground to a shrub and then to a clothesline.

They have clustered around my winter bird feeders and fought with each other over the seeds I have put out.

Once I dressed up my young daughters to go out to feed the birds in a special way. I had sacks of feed, and I thought that we would make 'snow angels' in the snow and then fill in the 'wings' and bodies and heads with the different colored seed I had. I had cracked corn and black sunflower and red millet! What a pretty way to feed the winter birds on a cold winter day!

We had fun! We wallowed around making snow angels with our bodies until we had several that we thought would work for our project. Then we filled in the spaces we had hollowed out with the seeds. Our angels looked marvelous!

We had made our angels on a slope where people who might be driving by would be able to see them. They were pretty the way they were, but we were anxious for the birds to find them and enjoy the seeds we had put out. Several days went by and the angels seemed undisturbed. The girls were disappointed.

On the third day we went into town for groceries, and as we returned we looked to see the angels, and the birds were there. It wasn't what we had pictured, though. The angels had been completely destroyed, seed shells were scattered about, and most of the birds seemed to be fighting each other over the remaining seeds. We were all surprised and disappointed. Somehow we had forgotten that the point of our project was to feed hungry birds, and, of course, the angels would be wrecked as the birds ate, and we should have expected that there would probably be a few squabbles among the hungry because their very survival depended upon that food.

We decided that we would do it again, sometime, even if it was a bit disconcerting to see our lovely angels torn apart. Things aren't always the way you picture them. The lovely angels were for us. The seeds were for the birds.

My mother loved birds. She kept a bird list of the first time she sighted different birds, and she treasured a huge volume of prints by Audubon, although I felt the little blue, bird-identification book we had was much more useful. She enjoyed having birds in her garden, and she always kept up feeders and bird baths in our yard.

She also liked to have pet birds. The first pet bird that I remember was a parakeet which I named Davy. His whole name was 'Davy Crackett' because I was much enamored with Davy Crockett at the time, and I thought that changing Crockett to Crackett was pretty clever.

Davy especially liked my father. We would let Davy out of his cage, and he would go right to my father and perch on his shoulder. Then he would move very carefully and slowly over to my father's ear and pluck out any stray hair that he might see. My brother and I found this to be hilarious, and we would howl with pleasure as my father would wince and then resume reading his newspaper.

Later, after Davy died, my mother chose a bird for her own pleasure. She had always loved to hear canaries sing, and one of her sisters had one that sang the most lovely trills. Her sister suggested a breeder, and my mother excitedly chose her bird. We didn't know that canaries sometimes need to be taught how to sing! It became a family project to coax our little friend to sing. Since none of us could trill like a canary, my mother bought a recording of canaries singing. I don't know if that record is how our bird learned to sing, or if he just decided that we were his family and that he would sing for us. Either way he did learn to sing and it was a delight to hear him. We kept our canary in a cozy little well lighted nook which we called 'the bird room'. My mother had every house plant imaginable in that room because of the light and the warmth there, and in the winter it was truly pleasant to hear the canary singing among the African violets, spider plants, flowering Hoyas, and begonias in that warm little spot.

Another bird came to live with us shortly before my mother died. A friend of the family gave my parents an African Grey Parrot. The parrot had been rescued—he was 'wild', outside in Indiana! No one had claimed him, and the people who had found him had kept him for several years but had grown tired of caring for him. My father's friend remembered that my family had had birds over the years, and he offered to get it for my father and mother. My mother was in a nursing home at the time and my father was living alone in the old house. He was delighted to have such a fascinating pet to befriend. My father swore me to secrecy about the parrot when he first got it, because he wanted to surprise my mother. We were planning on transporting her home for a day, and we thought that we would let her discover that the bird room had a new occupant. Unfortunately my mother wasn't feeling well, then developed pneumonia and died the very week that the parrot came to us.

My father grieved. At first he said, every time he looked at the parrot, "I never even told her about you!" Her sudden illness had been so traumatic that he had forgotten to mention that he had a surprise for her in the 'bird room'.

The parrot, Paul, and my father became good friends, and Paul helped my father survive his grief. Ten years later, when my father died, I inherited Paul. One day several months after my father died, I heard Paul whistling a tune that my father had taught him. He stopped suddenly and, because I knew the tune, I finished it by whistling back. I was in a different room at the time and when I came out of the room, I saw Paul attentively looking in my direction. Then as he saw me, he pulled back and slowly made his way down to the very bottom of his cage and then over to the farthest corner where he sat with his head down. I realized that he had thought that my father had magically returned. I hadn't realized that he had missed my father as much as I was missing him.

Missing people, missing things, missing…

******

If being by the water's edge and swimming were so important for me, why did I spend years holding myself away from the water? That is not so easy a question to answer. Why did Rapunzel waste away all those years in the desert? Why did Briar Rose sleep? In both of those cases, we are told that it happened because they were cursed. Both of them were judged disobedient and, also, both had been overcome with curiosity. And then, when you think about it, so was Snow White guilty of these sins! I suspect that many heroes and heroines of folk stories cross boundaries that have been laid out for them…And who is it that sets these boundaries? Is it always an old hag? Perhaps there is back story for the old hag, also.

I suspect, however, that these boundaries are erected in these somewhat arbitrary places because of some greater influence than can be found in an old hag. Boundaries are put down because of the rules and constraints of culture. Society can only perpetuate itself if everyone obeys the rules, and so rule-breakers are punished. Some die, some are exiled and ostracized, and some fall asleep. The rules and boundaries change only when there are more rule-breakers than there are rule-followers…at least that is my musing thought.

I stayed away from water because I was told that water and swimming were bad. I was ridiculed and warned, but I think I could have withstood that. What I couldn't withstand was what I thought was Reason. I married a man who claimed that swimming was unsanitary and bad for one's health and safety. Being near the edge of water was alright for adults, perhaps, but dangerous for children, and so why should anyone go near the water's edge? Water, after much sanitation and purifying, was for washing and drinking and served no other useful purpose. We had children together, and he reluctantly agreed that the children could have swimming lessons…as a safety precaution against…world flooding, I guess. I couldn't honestly and reasonably argue against him, because I knew first hand of the dangers to health and safety presented by proximity to water…but I wondered… he didn't seem to have such strong feelings about the other hazards of modern life. He didn't seem to feel that living in a polluted world of cars and airplanes and high speed trains and pesticides and Genetically Modified food and potent drugs was so dangerous that we should simply smother our offspring and be done with it.

And so I spent years away from water. Asleep in a glass coffin. Crumpled beside a spinning wheel. Waiting in a desert. Yes, waiting, like Rapunzel, in the furthest place one could be from water. When I began to awaken, I wondered if I could still swim. I signed up for swimming lessons and entered the pool with other adult students, many of whom were trying to overcome their fear of water.

"First, let's see how it feels to put your face in the water," the instructor said.

I put my face in the water, and I heard the water calling me. I heard its voice throbbing in my cells, in my blood, in my body. As my ears dipped deeper under the surface, I could hear my heart beat in the water, and I knew the Silkie had found her skin.

That summer of swimming lessons was an odd adventure. The instructors did not know what to make of me as I floated and cavorted among the frightened, water-shy beginners. I explained that I hadn't been swimming for years and that I had been afraid that I had forgotten how to swim…it sounded lame, but they accepted that, and I became an unofficial assistant, using my experiences with teaching children to overcome their fear of water and then to swim, to help those adults. At the end of the sessions one instructor said, "You know, I have never in my life seen someone who is as comfortable in water as you are!" For some reason, that one comment of validation pleased me. I knew I had been waiting in the wrong world.

And the 'backstory'? My husband had never learned how to swim, although he had always claimed that he had learned as a young teen. He also claimed that he couldn't risk getting into the water because of recurrent ear infections-which, of course, could have been the truth. But he had never said that he was terrified of the water. He never mentioned that he was embarrassed that he had never learned this skill which he could see was so easy for me, and rather than admit that fact to anyone else, especially me, he had chosen to rigidly oppose all swimming and water activities on what he felt were Reasonable Grounds...grounds that could not, with certainty and sweeping assurance, be challenged and defeated. I, like poor foolish Sally in "The Great Pumpkin", had accepted his stated reasons for all those years! The only time I had challenged it was to insist that my children learn to swim-- because I knew that, indeed, water can be dangerous. And I knew that there are health risks such as parasites, and bacteria...There are no guarantees. But then, where in the world are there guarantees except on TV?

There was a family who kept a large, extravagant cruiser at the boat dock where my father moored our much smaller cruiser. The family had a girl my age, a younger son and a toddler-aged daughter. The grandparents of the family actually owned the boat, but the younger family commandeered it almost every weekend. I would frequently ride with them as we traveled up and down the river, especially when my family and their family were headed toward the same destination. We children would play board games and card games together as we rode, and then, usually, at some point we would stop and swim. They generally liked to go to a place where there was a beach since they had a toddler. My family could stop almost anywhere and, as I was the primary swimmer, I would just jump overboard and swim midstream until my parents called me in, so we weren't bound by beaches.

At any rate, one summer as we were cruising together, and we children were taking turns riding in each other's boats, the young girl and I were busy making homemade paper dolls in our boat's cabin. I usually didn't do that sort of thing by myself, but enjoyed doing it with someone else. It surprised us that a speedboat came up to us to give us a message from the girl's family. They wanted her to come back because the boy had come down with something, and they were afraid that she might come down with it next and didn't want her to be feeling sick on our boat…plus they hoped that she hadn't accidently exposed us to something contagious. It rather put a damper on our outing, but I told her 'good-bye' and that I hoped that she didn't come down with anything. She left on the speedboat courier, and we continued down the river. When we got to our first destination, we visited with others who were there, but the big cruiser stayed at a distance. We heard that the little boy was pretty sick; that he had a fever and that they were trying to bring it down. My mother offered to send out aspirin, if they needed that as that was a standard medicine to bring down fever at that time. I was disappointed that my friend couldn't come and play, but I made the best of it and really wasn't very worried about it all. Later that night, however, the family left for the nearest river town with a dock large enough for their boat to be moored. The little boy was dangerously ill. My parents were alarmed as were all the parents. I think that everyone was thinking, 'polio'. It was summer. The polio vaccine was new, but I had had it.

I don't think I ever learned exactly what the diagnosis for his illness was. He had a fever that couldn't be broken, even in the hospital where he spent quite some time. He didn't die and to me that was most important. Somehow, although I had grown up in a small town where I had often encountered people who had been disabled or disfigured by disease, I had seen them as if they had always been that way, and not as victims, although survivors, of disease and injury. The only bad outcome of an illness or an accident was death, to me.

When my father and mother began to say that I couldn't swim in the river, because, it was believed that the little boy had picked up that illness from swimming in the polluted river, I was indignant. How could it be from the river? I thought that they were being very unfair, and I wanted to swim. I was sorry he had been sick, but now he was fine, and I thought that if he had caught that fever from the river, that since the rest of us hadn't caught it, well, we wouldn't catch it.

I don't know if my parents thought to plan what happened next or not, but it was effective as far as helping me to realize that there might be more to things than my shallow experiences had yet taught me. We went to visit the family from the big boat.

I remember that my parents told me that that family was not planning on returning to the boat docks and so, if we wanted to see them and say goodbye and wish them well, that we would need to spend a day driving to their home to visit. I was puzzled because I couldn't understand why they wouldn't come back to the river.

As it happened, we went to visit, and I was welcomed by my friend, and she happily led me to her room to see her dolls and toys. But her brother didn't seem to recognize me. He didn't seem to recognize anyone. Everyone else was strangely subdued and spoke in quiet tones. Even the toddler was quiet and poised as though waiting for something.

I followed my friend to her room, and she seemed relieved as she closed the door and shut the others out. She showed me her dolls, and I told her that she would probably like to see my dollhouse and that I had a collection of horses, too. I didn't mention my insects. As she was telling me about her dolls, she was naming them and then she came to a boy doll. She picked him up and said, "I don't even think he has a name, now. I don't think he knows his name anyway. He is dead." And then she threw him across the room.

I was startled. I had never had a dead doll. Then she ran across the room and without saying a word, she put him back on the shelf, and we finished our visit by playing "Go Fish" with a deck of cards that were shaped like fish.

When my parents were ready to leave they came to my friend's room and got me. We all hugged everyone except the little boy who still sat listlessly on the couch, wrapped in a blanket like a baby. My mother leaned over him and tried to say something to him, but he pulled away as though he was afraid of her. It was the only movement that I saw him make.

When we were back in the car, my mother said that she thought that he might get a little better because he had tried to move away from her. She thought that that movement might mean that he was still a little aware of the world around him. I was concerned about all that I had seen, but I didn't know what to ask or how to ask about it all. I must have said something, because I remember that my father told me that the fever had been so high for so long that much of the boy's brain had died of the heat. It was thought that he would never be the boy he had been.

I remember, suddenly, understanding why I couldn't swim in the river anymore that summer, and, maybe, never again.

Oh yes, I knew that water could carry diseases and change lives.

And I knew about the dangers of drowning. Once, I stood with some other children on the bank near the boat dock and watched as the Indiana University 'Showboat' came in to shore. It was quite a spectacle as the Showboat had a calliope and was filled with young adults, the actors, and they put on quite a show for anyone who might be watching. Our dock was privately owned and the Showboat had tried to pull into the public access area. I'm not certain if there was to be a performance that night or if the stop was merely for supplies of some type, or, perhaps, they were just stopping for the night as they made their way up and down the river. I was quite young. I mainly remember that it was getting pretty dark.

Some children from town had joined us boat dock children, and we were all just watching. I think that the Showboat people were having trouble getting secured. Anyway, there was some confusion and some of the bigger children kept going in and out of the water to try to help. I didn't even think about trying to help or going in the water, because I really didn't understand what was going on. The Showboat would start to drift out if they cut the engines, so the pilot kept revving up the engines to keep the boat close enough to the shore for the mooring lines to reach. The boys who were in the water, were up and down, laughing and shouting, and the young adults who were on the boat and also in and out of the water, were being pretty tolerant of their antics.

A little town girl who was standing near me suddenly took off, running up the hill to her home. I didn't think much about it because it was getting very dark, and, if I had thought about it, I would have assumed that she had to be home by dark, and that she was already late!

A few minutes later she returned with her mother who began screaming almost incoherently above the Showboat's engine and the noise of the boys and the students. The woman ran right into the water screaming and trying to get everyone's attention.

Her young son had been one of the boys who had gone into the water to help and, as his sister had stood there watching, he had gone under and then had never come up again. His sister had run all the way up the hill to get her mother and to tell her what had happened. The rest of us had stood there, unaware that a boy had drowned right in front of us…right as we stood there watching. My parents swooped down on my brother and me like eagles and hurried us off to our boat and away from the shocked chaos that ensued as the realization of what had happened swept over the boat landing.

The Showboat engines were cut, the calliope stopped, of course, and the children on the shore were sent home or moved up onto the bank to stand with their parents. From our boat I could hear the much subdued sounds of the men, now helped by the local police as they searched for the boy's body. I imagined that they would find him and somehow bring him back to life, the way I thought adults could do. My parents made me go to bed, but I could see the flash of the revolving red light of the police car which was parked on the bank above us. I knew when they found the boy because it became very quiet outside, except for the sobbing of the mother, and then the red light stopped flashing in our window and the police car and the other emergency cars and trucks left up the hill, one by one.

And once, on Christmas day, my girlfriend called me and asked if I wanted to go ice skating with her on a near-by lake. We had been going ice skating there for several days, and she had been borrowing my mother's skates, because she didn't have her own. This time she was excited, because that morning she had opened her presents, and she had gotten her own pair of skates. I was torn because I wanted to see her new skates, and it did sound like it would be fun to head out to the lake and get some fresh air after a candy and hot chocolate-filled morning.

Her brothers had said that they would take us, as they wanted to play hockey, and she and I could just enjoy skating while they played. I knew my mother would be disappointed if I went, though, because we had not had our Christmas dinner yet, and I was pretty certain that to even ask if I could go would hurt my mother's feelings. I could hear her bustling around in the kitchen trying to put together the perfect holiday meal. I told my friend that we hadn't eaten our special dinner yet, and that I felt like I should stay home with my family on

Christmas Day. I said that I would ask my Dad if he would take us to the lake the next day, and that I was excited to see her new skates. Later that afternoon, after finishing our holiday meal and helping with the dishes, I was feeling rather dejected about missing out on the ice-skating. The house seemed too warm and the smell of all that holiday food on a very full stomach, and all those sweet things…all put together made me feel a little cranky and blue, but I was trying to hide it.

Then the fire siren went off. We all looked at my father, who was a volunteer fireman.

"Oh, don't go!" My mother cried to my father. "You always go. It's Christmas, and I wanted us to have a cozy day, all day!"

My father just shrugged as he finished pulling on his warmest gear. "Someone isn't having a good Christmas right now, and we have had a wonderful day, so far. I have to go, it could be a house fire because of tree lights, you know."

My mother nodded. She knew he would go. Every time the siren went off, no matter what time of night, first I would wake to the siren, and then I would hear my father's feet hit the floor, next I would hear him running down the stairs and finally, I would hear the slam of the front door. We lived only a block away from the fire station, and he was usually the first person there. He would throw open the big station doors and get the engines ready to answer the call.

He left, and I went back to my quiet activities and my somber mood.

When the telephone rang a short time later, I didn't bother to run and answer, because I thought it would be one of my mother's relatives calling to wish us "Merry Christmas". I heard my mother gasp and then she said, "Oh no!" I was surprised when she then turned to me and said, after a pause, that the call was for me. I went to the phone and discovered that it was a girl my age from up the street. She had heard what the fire call was about from a friend whose father was also a fireman, and she had been told that a girl had gone through the ice at the lake and that no one could get to her and that she had drowned. She knew that I went out to the lake to skate, and she had been wondering if it had been me. She finally had decided to call, because she thought if we answered, then she would know that it wasn't me…

I told her about my earlier invitation to go skate and that my friend, our classmate, had gotten new skates and had planned to go to the lake with her brothers, but that I thought that they surely would have gone and would have been home long before now. I remember the silence on the phone line as we both thought this over. Then I told her that I would let her know what my father said when he got home.

I didn't call her back that night, though. My father came home and avoided me at first. My friend had drowned. While her brothers were busy playing hockey, she had skated out on the lake alone. Apparently there were ducks roosting on the ice in one spot, and she had headed over toward them, never supposing that the ice might have been thinner where the ducks had been.

Her sharp new skates had taken her far across the thin ice as it cracked beneath her, and she had gone under with barely a cry to alert her brothers. When they saw what had happened, they had gone toward her and had tried to reach the spot where she had gone through. They had tried to lie down and form a chain and use their hockey sticks to reach the gaping hole where she might have been, but they had failed. My father and the other fireman had finally found her. The weight of her warm clothes and the new skates had pulled her under the frigid water. I overheard my father tell my mother that she mustn't tell anyone, but that they had had to use grappling hooks to retrieve her body. My father was in shock. He never mentioned that last bit of information to me. He would only say that it was a heartbreaking experience and that he and the other men who had been there would never forget it.

I never mentioned what I had overheard. I wondered if my friend would have gone over toward those ducks if I had been there. If I had been there, we might not have done that because we would have been busy with our own games. Still, I thought, we might have gone over there out of curiosity or just to see the ducks fly up! I might have even been the one who suggested that we 'go exploring' and have led the way. I don't think it would have occurred to me that there could be thinner ice under those ducks, either. Oh, I know something about the dangers of water.

******

I don't recall a duck in Rapunzel's story, but ducks are mentioned in several other fairy tales and in many folk tales. They are usually helpful creatures. They don't usually lure people to their death, although I do know of a story, "Fundevogel", where the girl in the story asks the boy to turn himself into a pond, and she, then, turns herself into a duck and when the witch, who is a cook in the story, leans down to get a drink, the duck grabs her head and holds her under the water…But it was a witch, a cook who has plotted to murder the little boy. The duck/girl was being helpful to drown the witch/cook, but for me, the imagery of the duck and a person being held under water until they drown arouses contradictory feelings. I prefer to focus on the other aspects of ducks. Helpful ducks. In Hansel and Gretel a duck ferries the children, one at a time, across the lake so that they can return home after their triumph over the witch. I feel better.

And we have come to some duck stories. One Easter, when I was a young married woman with young children, and we all lived in a rented farmhouse, I asked our landlord, privately if he knew of anyone who could get us a duckling for the children for Easter. I had in mind a fluffy, little creature who could be a pet. My landlord had quite a different picture in his mind. He assured me that he knew someone who had ducks, and that he could get one for me.

I was pleased because we had not had any pets except an inside cat, and I thought the children would be excited about a little duck as a pet. A few days before Easter, the landlord called with what I thought at the time was a rather strange question. He said that the farmer who had the duck wanted to know if I wanted it dead or alive.

"Oh!" I said, "I want it alive! Just a little duckling for the children…for Easter."

My landlord hesitated and said, "So you will take care of it yourself?"

"Oh, yes. Just bring it here, and I will take care of it," I answered. I was beginning to feel a little uneasy. Something didn't seem quite right about this conversation, but I didn't want to embarrass our landlord. We had just moved onto the farm, and we didn't know him very well.

Our landlord asked, "So when should I bring it over for you?"

I said, "It would be best if you brought it over on Saturday evening so the children don't see it."

"On Saturday? Right before Easter Sunday? Saturday night?" he asked.

"Yes. Will that work out for you?" I quizzed.

"Oh," and he hesitated, then added, "I think so. I will bring it over in a box and put it in the laundry room for you."

"That should work for me! Thank you for doing this for me! Let me know what I owe you for the duckling!" I added, thinking, perhaps that the money issue was the problem that I thought I could detect in his voice.

"Oh well, it will be about three dollars, I think. I'll get the bill for it for you," he said, and he did sound a little more assured.

On Saturday I was busy all day. I had boiled eggs for the children to color, and I had set up a place for them to dip the eggs in the dye. I had done some baking and had our Easter dinner all planned. The house was tidy except where the children had arranged their Easter baskets and had filled them with the commercial Easter grass. Our family tradition included a basket hunt inside the house with baskets for each child filled and hidden by the Easter Bunny, and an egg hunt for the colored eggs that the Bunny hid outside in the yard.

The children were excited and were restless. It took me a while to get them settled. I heard our landlord's truck pull in the driveway, and I heard the outside door into our laundry room/mudroom open and close. I could hardly wait to get downstairs and sneak a peek at the duckling, but I tried to act as normally as possible. I read stories and tucked each child in as quickly as my husband got them dried off from their baths.

Finally we both managed to get back downstairs. I posted myself at the base of the stairs in order to stop any straggler child who might try to come downstairs on some pretence, while my husband went outside to be certain the back door was shut …and to check on the duckling.

When he came back in, he was frowning. I was puzzled.

"What's wrong? Doesn't it look healthy? It is alive, isn't it?" I asked, suddenly remembering our landlord's question.

"Oh yes, it is alive. I just don't think it is what you had in mind," my husband said in a low voice. Then he added, "I think it is mean, too."

I was mystified. A mean duckling?

I traded my 'post' at the base of the stairs with him and scampered out to the laundry room. There was a very large cardboard box sitting by the washing machine. As soon as I closed the door between the kitchen and the laundry, I heard something move in the box. It sounded like a large rat, scrabbling away inside the box. Then it was quiet. I moved closer to the box and carefully opened one of the top flaps. I was greeted by much hissing and a sudden chaotic thrashing of something inside the box. I caught a glimpse of one bright, beady eye and then a lot of feathers. I quickly closed up the box the way it had been closed.

It wasn't a darling little duckling. It was a full grown duck. A duck in a box. An angry duck in a box. Now I understood what I had heard in my landlord's voice. He was wondering how I could butcher and pluck and prepare a duck for Easter dinner so quickly. Apparently he didn't live in a world where children are given ducklings or chicks or baby bunnies at Easter. Or, perhaps, because I was a 'renter', he didn't think that I lived in that chicky, ducky world!

I turned off the light in the laundry and returned to the kitchen where I reassured my husband that I could deal with this disappointment. I promptly got a bad case of the giggles. We continued with our holiday preparations and then we turned off all of the lights and went to bed.

The morning started early as the children were eager to search for their baskets in the house so that they could discover just what the Bunny had left for them. Each child had specific baskets to find and the rule was that if you found someone else's basket, you weren't to tell them. Only when someone had a basket that they simply couldn't find could you offer hints. Usually we used the 'warmer, warmer, colder, colder' method in order to help the searcher. As usual, this basket search took up the better part of an hour, and then everyone spent some time examining the contents of the baskets. There were a few simple toys... balsa wood airplanes to put together and fly outside, and paddle ball sets—and, of course, there was candy...marshmallow eggs and bunnies, chocolate covered eggs with various fillings, and jelly beans.

We grown-ups had coffee, and croissants with butter and jam, while we watched the children. Finally it was time to move everyone outside for the outside egg hunt. It was a cool morning , and so I suggested that our oldest son, who was about six at the time, go outside quickly and see if we needed to put on our coats or if we just needed to wear sweatshirts.

He scampered out the door into the laundry room; and, presumably went on outside to check on the temperature. I was busy dressing the younger children and wiping chocolate off of their faces. Our son came back into the kitchen a few minutes later and said nothing. Everyone was struggling to put on jeans and shoes and to choose which basket each would use to gather eggs. Our son still said nothing.

"What is it like outside?" I asked.

Our son shrugged and fiddled with a basket that he was considering for the egg hunt.

"Should we get coats?" our daughter asked innocently.

Our son shrugged again. Our toddler boy ran to the laundry room door with his chosen basket and, at that, our older son leapt to his feet and threw himself between his baby brother and the door. He cried out, "No!! You can't go out there!"

We all stopped abruptly and stared at him!

"You can't go because there is a monster in a box out there and it is going 'hisssssss' and the box is moving all around" he sobbed.

I couldn't resist the opportunity to make this moment into an adventure. "Oh no!" I cried. "You must be mistaken! What kind of monster could be in a box in our laundry room? Maybe if we are all very quiet we can just take a peek and see!"

My husband and I crept over to the door and carefully opened it a bit. The box had moved from the night before, but it was quiet…no hissing. We closed the door, and I reported to our wide-eyed audience, "There is a very large box out there, but at this moment there is no hissing coming from it."

"How will we get outside to look for eggs?" our daughter asked.

"What if the box monster ate the eggs!" my husband offered.

Everyone looked shocked at that suggestion.

I opened the door a crack, peeked out again, and then I bravely said, "I will go closer to the box, but if there is hissing, I will come right back, so keep the door open for me!" Then I tiptoed out toward the box and bravely opened the top. The duck went berserk. He started hissing and flapping his wings. The children screamed and my husband burst out laughing as the frightened duck scrambled out of the box and into the laundry room. I leapt backward to guard the door so he couldn't flap his way into the kitchen just as my husband closed me in the laundry room with the angry duck. I turned to see him holding the children, one after another to look through the little window in the upper part of the door so they could see that I was okay and that the monster was really a large male mallard duck.

When everyone was convinced that it was safe, one-by-one, they joined me in the laundry room. I had subdued our monster and was holding him. The children quickly learned that ducks don't have teeth, and that once you know what is making that terrifying noise, it isn't so terrifying. Our son was glad to know that his father had thought that the duck sounded mean, too.

I asked the children what they thought we should name the duck who had come to live with us. They decided to name him 'Snarl'!

Snarl was too big to keep in a box in the laundry room, so we fixed up a place in an abandoned chicken coop in the farmyard. We covered all the openings with chicken wire and rigged up a run for him. Then we dragged out an old children's swimming pool and filled it with water for him. That turned out to be the hardest part of our duck care routine. Snarl dirtied up that water pretty fast.

The children figured out that we could put a small cat collar around Snarl's neck and then they could take turns walking him around the yard with a leash. At first this was pretty tame. Snarl would walk this way and that and the child would follow his lead. Sometimes the child would try to lead Snarl, but that was difficult because if Snarl didn't want to go the way they wanted to go, well, they were afraid they would break his neck, so they usually just called for help and someone else would come over and try to herd Snarl in the chosen direction.

After a month or so, Snarl got even larger and stronger, and the daily walks were even funnier to watch. Our children were almost dragged around the yard as they tried to walk Snarl. It took two children holding on to the leash to keep Snarl in line. Sometimes, our various neighbors would drive slowly by watching our children walking their duck on a leash in the yard. Once when the neighbor slowed down and then honked and waved, Snarl bolted. He opened his wings and began to beat them as he broke into a run. The children were startled and awkwardly ran and stumbled, hanging on to that leash as they went back and forth across the yard. Finally Snarl settled down and the children got him back into his pen.

I found out later that Snarl's walks were the talk of the neighborhood. Everyone for five miles around drove by to see if they could catch a glimpse of the city folk's children walking a big mallard on a leash. One neighbor finally asked me why we had the duck on a leash. I said, "So he won't run away!"

She sat me down and explained that the furthest the duck would go would be down to the creek for a swim, and then he would return to the place where you fed him and where he roosted for the night.

We still filled the little swimming pool now and then, because it was fun to see him splash and play in it…but the leash walks became very rare.

I had had a pet duck when I was a child, but my duck came to me as a small duckling. It also came as a rather strange gift after a rather strange experience.

It was summer, and I was going to go to a summer camp for two weeks. At the same time that I was to be gone, my parents and my brother were headed out for a long boat trip down the Kentucky River with some other boating enthusiasts.

I spent the night with some friends of my parents, Lou and Ralph. Lou, short for LuluBelle, was going to manage the store while my parents and my grandfather, who was visiting my aunt, were out of town. Lou and Ralph were to take me to the home of another family whom I didn't know at all, who were going to take me to camp as they were driving across the state to take their son to the same camp. I was perfectly comfortable with the rather haphazardness of this plan. It was similar to most of my family's plans. Rather fairytale-ish.

At any rate the plan seemed to be falling into place. I waved goodbye to my brother and my parents as they left for their trip, and I was swept up by my parent's friends and taken to their house for the night. I was a little shy about it all, but I knew them and although the food for supper was decidedly different from what we usually ate at home, it was good and filling and then I was tucked in rather awkwardly, because they had only had one child and that one was a boy who was even older than my brother, and they were unsure about little girls...and maybe they were expecting me to be homesick, or nervous about camp. Anyway, I remember it as being a little awkward, but I went right to sleep and then, in the morning, I woke up and got dressed to go to meet the people who would be taking me to camp.

We drove to the next town and endured a rather discombobulated set of introductions as LuluBelle had to explain that she and Ralph weren't my parents, or any sort of relation, and the people had to explain that their son was refusing to go to the camp, but since I was expecting them to take me there, and they had paid for their son to go, that we would make the trip to the camp and hopefully both of us, the children, would stay there.

It seemed a bit troubling, but I was still undaunted. I was introduced to the boy who was decidedly unpleasant toward me. I didn't think of it then, but I realize now, that if it weren't for me, he probably would have gotten his parents to give in and let him stay home. I really think that his parents did not want to make the trip and were hoping that my parents would just take me to camp…but since I was delivered by people who weren't even my parents, well…

And so I was shuffled into the backseat of an unfamiliar family car with a hostile boy who refused to speak to me and pinched me at every opportunity. We rode in that car for hours. The boy's mother and father tried to talk to me, and I eagerly answered their questions about why I liked camp and such, but that brought on more pinching, but I hated to tell on that boy. I could sense that this family was even more strange than my own family, although I never would have described my family that way at that time. This family was not just strange, but also uncomfortable.

Hours. We drove for hours. I watched the scenery as I pressed myself as close to the door as possible in order to escape Mr. Pinchy. I wished that I hadn't packed my books in my suitcase which was in the trunk. I began to feel hopeful and excited as we finally got closer to the camp entrance.

Then, disaster!! There was a man waiting at the entrance to the camp. He was stopping each car, saying something to each of them, and then motioning them to turn around. Other cars were leaving. When the man got to us, he told us that the water main had broken, and that the camp for this two week period was cancelled. Our money would be refunded. The boy's father asked why we hadn't been called as we had driven three hours to get there, and it seemed inconsiderate not to have called us.

The man said that the water main had broken that morning and that there had been no time to call all the campers. Besides that, at first they had thought that they would be able to fix the break. At any rate, we had to go home.

As if the drive over hadn't been bad enough, the drive home was much worse. I was terribly disappointed. I had given up a river trip for nothing. I kept thinking that somehow, everything would suddenly be fixed, and we would be called to come back. Then I realized that the camp would have to call this family in order to tell me because…no one was home at my house. And then I thought…no one is home at my house. I imagined what it would be like to stay in my house all by myself. I wasn't pleased with this thought. Then I thought about staying with this family for the two weeks. That was an even worse thought.

To make matters worse, the boy was obviously delighted that the camp was shut down. He was enjoying what he perceived as a victory over his parents, and his parents knew that. His father was fuming. He obviously resented the fact that fate had favored his son. The boy's mother attempted to console me by saying, "I suppose that you are disappointed about this."

I managed to choke out that, yes, I was disappointed, and Mr. Smirky laughed a snorty little laugh. The atmosphere in the car had gone from noxious to poisonous, and, then, at some point in the long ride home, someone in the front seat realized that they didn't know where to take me.

"So where are your parents?" I was asked.

"Somewhere on a boat along the Ohio, or maybe the Kentucky River," I answered.

"Well, we need to get a hold of them so they can come and get you. Did they tell you how to reach them?"

Of course, they hadn't told me anything like that. It hadn't occurred to them that this marvelous plan might collapse.

When I didn't answer, they asked me about relatives.

"I have an aunt in Colorado, and some other relatives somewhere far away in Ohio. We don't see them very often because they live so far away," I offered.

"What about the people who brought you to our house?" the boy's mother asked.

I was beginning to feel badly about my family. My family didn't seem to be a very good family. I was beginning to feel abandoned.

I told the boy's parents that I could go to my parents' friends' house and that they would probably know how to reach my parents. That seemed to mollify the boy's parents for a while. It didn't mollify me, though. I knew that Lou and Ralph were not going to know how to reach my parents. The whole point of the Kentucky River trip was that it was an adventure. No one went that far up the river anymore. It was really isolated, and my parents and their friends had discussed this. They had agreed that it was a chance they were willing to take, since it was unlikely that anything would happen to anyone in the time that they would be gone. And Lou and Ralph had agreed that they could handle an emergency as that was an unlikely event anyway.

We finally reached the boy's house, and his father carried my luggage up to the porch and left it there. I was at a loss as to what was expected of me, so I sat down on my sleeping bag. At least I had something to sleep in, I thought…and clothes. The family didn't have Lou and Ralph's phone number, and I didn't know it, but as it was still before closing time at the store, I told them to call the store. I knew the number for that at least.

The boy's mother called and then came to tell me that someone would be picking me up. They offered me dinner, but I declined although I was starving. I said I would just wait for my ride outside on the porch. I sat back down on my sleeping bag. I could hear a royal knock-down, drag out fight going on inside the house between the boy and his father, and I didn't want to be a witness to murder as well as being an orphan and abandoned, and having the world's worse parents.

When Lou arrived, I could tell that she wasn't happy. I think that running the store was as much as she had planned on doing while my parents were gone. She had always said that she had wanted a little girl, but she didn't seem to want one now. Or maybe it was Ralph who didn't want a little girl around. Or maybe it was just that since both of them worked, I would have to stay at their house alone or go to the store with LuluBelle. I didn't really know, but I could sense that my need for a place to stay was a distinct inconvenience.

At any rate, I went home with Lou and ate a quiet dinner with her family, endured some teasing by Lou and Ralph's son about how I liked their house so well that I had decided to come back, and then went to bed. This time I was homesick although I didn't let them know.

In the morning, I slept late. It was a Sunday and so Lou did not have to go into town to open the store. She had made a big breakfast which I had missed, but which she warmed up for me. Then she told me that my uncle was coming to get me. I would be spending the time that my parents were gone with my uncle, his thin wife and my three girl cousins.

I was shocked. I said, "But they live so far away!"

Lou was quiet. She watched me as she took a draw on her cigarette. "No," she said, "they just live about twenty miles from here. I got their phone number from the directory. They are your relatives that live the closest to here. That is why I called them. I thought you should be with relatives while your folks are gone."

This was news to me. I was remembering how long a drive it had been the time we had gone to visit them. I was remembering that we never saw them, 'because they were so far away'. And I remembered my father and the gun and the squirrel. My anxiety level moved up the chart quite a way, but what could I do? At least I would see Racky and Juanita. Maybe it would be fun.

My uncle came to get me in an old farm truck. He wasn't pleased.

"Where'yer folks?" He asked me.

"On a boat trip up the Kentucky River," I answered as we bounced along on a narrow gravel road between two barb wire fences which were holding in rows of young corn.

"Why aren't you with them? Why didn't they make better arrangements for you? I'm losing a whole day here, fetching you!" he grumbled at me.

I wondered if he was really losing a whole day. Lou had said he was close by and, anyway, it was Sunday. Most of the farmers I knew only worked on Sundays during the planting and the harvest. I was afraid to argue with him, though. I looked at him from the side and his face looked rock hard and his mouth was held in a tight line. I just sat quietly hanging on to the seat as best as I could.

We came up on the farm from a different direction than we had come when my parents had come. It really wasn't so very far away. My uncle never said another thing until he had stopped the truck and gotten out. As I was struggling to get out my door he pulled my suitcase and sleeping bag out of the truck and dropped them to the ground. "Take your things on into the house", he said as he turned toward the barn and strode off.

I was dragging my suitcase while trying to keep my sleeping bag off the ground and making my way slowly toward the front porch of the house, when Martha bustled out of the house to help me. She took the suitcase, and we both maneuvered our way up the front steps, onto the porch and into the front room. The room was darker than I remembered, but I could smell something cooking in the kitchen, and that made me feel a little better. I wondered where Juanita was.

Martha put my suitcase down at the bottom of the stairs and turned to me, "Mom says that you and Juanita can sleep together, so she can show you where, when she comes up to the house. She's in the barn now. You come on in the kitchen. We are about ready to eat dinner. I'm glad Dad got you so fast. He gets grumpy if he doesn't eat on time."

I wondered just how much grumpier he could get. I figured that he must already be hungry for his dinner.

The kitchen was hot. The windows were open but there wasn't much of a breeze coming in. My aunt was busy stirring something on the stove. She had a smudged apron on over what looked like a nicer dress. She was wearing stockings and black shoes that looked a little old-fashioned, but sturdy. They didn't look like shoes to wear on a farm, though. She turned and smiled at me. "I'm making gravy," she explained. "Now tell me what happened that you aren't with your folks. I can't imagine they are going to be very happy to hear about this mix-up!"

She, at least, made me feel a little better about my situation. She didn't sound like she thought that my parents had just gone off on a lark and forgotten all about me. I almost felt like crying because I was so grateful to her. She turned back to her gravy, and I gave her a short version of the adventures of the last two days. Barbara, the oldest sister, came into the room and she and Martha kept exchanging looks while I told my story. My aunt motioned to both girls, and they quickly and quietly finished taking things out to the dining room table, and they set a place for me and pulled up an extra chair.

Juanita and my uncle came in through the mudroom. Both of them looked freshly washed up, but neither of them was as dressed up as my aunt and my other cousins looked to be. Juanita had on trousers and a loose shirt and my uncle had on the same bib overalls that he had worn to drive over to get me.

Before we ate, my uncle said a long 'grace'. I wasn't used to saying grace before meals, even on Sundays. In the summer we almost never attended church, because we were on the boat. I didn't think that my family was irreligious, however. I thought that we were Christians, just not church people. I knew to be quiet during grace, though.

We ate the rest of the meal almost in total silence. The only comment made was when my uncle asked if my cousins and aunt had enjoyed going to church that morning, to which they all said, very dutifully, "Yes". Nothing more was said until my aunt served dessert. It was then that Juanita turned to me and asked the question that must have been burning in her pocket throughout the whole meal.

"How come you are here getting to stay with us?" she asked.

So I got to tell the whole story again. My uncle left the table to read his newspaper and put up his feet a while, and the older girls began to clear the table around Juanita and myself. From that moment on Juanita and I became inseparable. I was

121

more her type anyway. I liked being outside and around animals, and I wasn't interested in the inside-of-a-house things like sewing or cooking.

For most of the next week Juanita had a little shadow behind her. I learned how to string fence, feed livestock, milk cows, and tend chickens. I was not strong enough to do half of those jobs, but I tried, and at least I saw how they were done. I stayed out of my uncle's way. He barely said a word to me.

The crisis came toward the end of the week. We had all come in for supper and my uncle had turned on a radio. He had done that other evenings, but I had not paid much attention to it. It seemed to be some radio preacher and for me it was just background yap.

This particular night I was very tired. We had been busy all day because the weather forecast was for storms and the animals were very restless. Milking had been a trial. Even the cats were fighting each other instead of waiting patiently for their share of the milk.

At any rate, I committed a mortal sin. I asked for someone to please pass the butter.

My uncle bellowed and rose out of his chair like a volcano exploding. His chair fell backwards, and my aunt moved from her chair beside him to be a bit in his path as he focused his look on me. I felt Juanita grab the collar of my shirt and yank me out of my chair, then we flew across the room, up the stairs, and into our bedroom where Juanita quickly pushed out the screen from the window and shoved me out onto the roof of the little porch that was right below her window. She quickly followed and then replaced the screen while motioning to me to flatten myself against the outside of the house. I could hear my uncle bellowing something as he was making his way up the stairs…obviously the cousins and my aunt had discreetly moved into his path and impeded his progress.

I was terrified, but Juanita seemed to have a plan. She pressed herself against the house on the other side of the window and then signaled to me to be perfectly quiet. I was willing to do that as I think I had stopped breathing already.

My uncle reached the window and bellowed out, "So you think you're smart!" Then he asked someone behind him to get his hammer and a few nails. Then he slammed the window shut. I looked across at Juanita. I guessed that my uncle hadn't tried to crawl out the window to get us because the window was a little attic sized window which we could get through, but he was a big, broad shouldered man, and he would have looked foolish trying to push through it…and I think that looking foolish was not something he felt like doing. A few minutes passed, and I was beginning to breathe again. I began to wonder what would happen next.

There was the sound of hammering from inside. As I looked across at Juanita, I saw that she was frowning. She was also watching the sky. It was getting darker outside, but the real reason she was looking at the sky was the storm that we had waited for all day was finally approaching. The sky beyond the barn was darkening rapidly and there were flashes of light. I heard the first faint rumble of thunder.

We stayed pressed against the house for a while longer. The hammering had stopped, but we could still feel my uncle's presence. Finally, as the first big drops of rain began to hit the roof, we heard the slam of the bedroom door. Juanita cautiously crept over to look at the window. "He nailed it shut!" she exclaimed. "Boy, you really got him going!"

"What did I do?" I asked.

"You asked for something during a prayer. Didn't you notice?"

Of course I hadn't noticed. I thought we were eating dinner, not attending church. It hadn't even occurred to me to pay attention to the radio preacher.

By now the rain was getting heavier and the thunder was louder and the lightening was closer. "Are you scared of weather?" Juanita asked.

"Not really," I answered.

"That's good, cause we are stuck here for a while, I think. I sometimes get down off this roof by hanging on to the trellis, but it is full of roses just now and, anyway, the overhang here might be better cover for us until the storm goes past. Might as well just hunker down a while." She moved herself flat up against the outside of the house again and squatted down.

The rain was coming down hard and the front side of my clothes was already soaked, but the storm seemed to be moving pretty fast. I looked out over the farm from this high perch and felt a little dizzy. The lightening was streaking down and the thunder shook the old house beneath me. After a few minutes the storm settled into a steady rain as the thunder and lightning and the roiling clouds and wind moved on. We sat crouched on the roof, silent, until the rain also began to lighten up and then a break in the clouds revealed a piece of the moon. I don't know how long we were there. It seemed like it was most of the night. My legs ached, and as the temperature dipped after the storm moved through, I was feeling cold.

"Well," Juanita broke the silence, "I think I will check the trellis. I've been thinking. Maybe if I can get down I can get a ladder and help you get down."

"You mean no one is going to open the window for us?" I whimpered in disbelief.

Juanita looked at me and replied, "Course not! We got ourselves into this. We got to get ourselves out of it."

I began to fight back tears. I was just too cold, and a lump had been in my throat during the whole storm, and I had been as brave as I could be, but the thought that someone, even, maybe my uncle, would rescue us had kept me going. No one? Not my aunt or my two inside girl cousins? Not my uncle coming to realize that I hadn't meant to cause a problem and that maybe he was being a bit too harsh?

"Don't cry. You've done good. You are stronger than you look and tougher. I'll get us off this roof. Don't worry."

With that she moved carefully out onto the roof. She sat a minute, as if thinking, and then removed her shoes and socks, stuffed her socks into the shoes, knotted the shoelaces together, and slung them over her shoulder. Then she crept closer to the edge and carefully turned around onto her stomach and felt with her feet until she found her footing on the trellis. She grimaced, and so I imagined that the briars on the roses were scratching her feet. She slowly edged down and then she pushed back and jumped to the ground with a thud.

I sucked in my breath as I listened, frozen in my spot. What if she was hurt? What could I do? A minute later I could make out her figure in the growing moonlight as she waved to me from further away from the house. She turned and loped off to the barn.

She got me down from my tower. She didn't use any magic hair, just guts. My hair was wet and limp and certainly not magic. I didn't fall into the briars. But Juanita's feet were pretty well cut up.

For the next several days we hid out in the woods that followed the creek that ran through the farm. Juanita had gotten us dry clothes from the stash of what she called 'barn clothes'. There hadn't been anything my size, but we just hiked up what she found for me with baling twine. And she had gotten matches and some old horse blankets. I wasn't missing out on camp after all, although when I thought of the neat and tidy cabins and the organized life of summer camp, I had to giggle.

We were having a little trouble with food, though. Martha had smuggled out some sandwiches and things for us when she took out slops for the hogs, and Juanita had managed to milk one of the cows a little early. We also tried our hand at gathering food from the woods. I caught some grasshoppers, and we decided to try toasting them, as Juanita assured me that people in other countries ate them, and I had read that fact somewhere myself. We built a little fire and speared our grasshoppers on sharpened sticks. After an exchange of looks which fed our resolve, we ate them. It wasn't a very good experiment though, as we discovered that not only did they not taste good, their back legs were very scratchy. Juanita wished for her gun as she was certain that we could get a rabbit and cook it…

We watched the farmhouse from a distance. Martha and Barbara were taking Juanita's place doing the barn chores. Juanita thought that that was funny as neither of the older girls liked that type of work, although they both had started out helping their Dad and then moved inside to help their mother as they got older and more 'female'. Juanita was determined that she would never grow female and end up doing inside jobs.

Finally, one afternoon after two or maybe three days out in the woods, we saw the old truck leave the farmyard. Juanita was excited. "Finally Dad's going to town!" she exclaimed.

She grabbed up our makeshift camp blankets and ran toward the house. Barbara and Martha and their mother came out the backdoor and stood in the yard, shading their eyes and looking out toward the woods, then waved to us, when they saw us coming.

"Get in the house and get washed up and changed," my aunt instructed.

I didn't need a second order. Martha said, "I've got some hot dish and biscuits for you after you're cleaned up."

Juanita and I shed our dirty, barn clothes, and Barbara gathered them to take to wash, or, maybe, to throw out. We showered and washed our hair and then I got into my own jeans and clothes. I wasn't sure if I should be packing more things to take back to the woods or not, but when Juanita saw me rooting through my things, she said, "No need. He's over it. He just went to town to give us a chance to get in and get back to normal."

I was puzzled. I expected a lecture and, probably, a demand for an apology at least.

When we got downstairs, there was food on the table which we ate with pleasure. I kept expecting someone to say something about the whole episode, but the only conversation was as though we had been gone out of town for a few days on business or something. Juanita finished eating and said, "Well, do you think I should fix that chicken feeder?"

Her mother paused and said, "That would be a good thing to do. Do it there in the yard so it's real obvious that you are working on it."

And that is what we were doing when my uncle drove back into the farmyard.

He parked the truck and swung out of the seat, looked at us a minute, then said, "You should use some of that wire I saved over behind the shed, then come get the milking done." Then he turned and walked out to the barn to start the rest of the evening chores.

We ate in silence at dinner. I made sure I knew when the radio preacher was praying.

When we got up to the room, I noticed that the window was open. I went over and looked out toward the barn. The ground looked very far down. I looked to see if I could see the nail holes. They were there. I hadn't imagined it all. I looked at Juanita, but she just shrugged.

A few days later, my parents drove up the lane. I was helping with the chickens and the ducks at the time, and so I saw them right away. My father parked the car. My parents both got out, and I saw my mother's face as she looked toward the farmhouse. I had never seen a look like that on her face before. She was as white as a ghost and her face was set like stone. She began to walk at a brisk place toward the house, but I called to her. She turned, and I ran to her and jumped up to hug her.

"Are you alright?" she asked.

"Sure," I said. "I'm helping with the ducks and chickens. Juanita has fixed up a new feeder for them. Come see!"

By this time my uncle and aunt were there as well as my father. My aunt said, "You heard about the camp?"

My mother nodded and wiped her eyes.

My uncle said, "Its fine, Mary Margaret. We took care of her."

"Come into the house and have some coffee," my aunt said. She turned to Juanita and me and said, "I have cookies made, too. You two wash up first, though."

We cleaned up from the job we had been doing and then washed up at the pump and went in the house through the mudroom. I heard my parents and my aunt and uncle talking as if nothing odd had happened at all. They laughed at some story or joke.

When we came in, my father said, "Have your cookies and then get your things together. Your brother is at Lou and Ralph's house, and we have to stop and pick him up before we go home."

I nodded. Juanita and I got our cookies and lemonade and sat down at the table. Martha and Barbara came over to me and said, "It was nice to have you stay a while." And they patted me on the back. I felt happy.

Juanita helped me pack my things. As we went to leave the room, I went over to the window again. The nail holes were still there. Again I looked at Juanita, but this time she just said, "We had fun, didn't we."

I nodded. I didn't want her to know how frightened I had been.

When all of my things were in the car and my mother had hugged everyone and my father had shaken hands, I gave my aunt and cousins a hug, and then I went up to my uncle and gave him a hug. As he leaned over, I gave him a kiss on the cheek.

When I turned to get into the car, my uncle said, "Wait a minute. I've got something for you." He turned and hurried off toward the back of the house, and then he came back with a box. "Close your eyes," he said.

I closed my eyes, and I heard him put something in the box. He put the box in the backseat of our car. "Now, you can get in the car and look in the box,"

I did as he said. I carefully opened the box and there inside was a duckling. It had yellow and black downy feathery fluff all over and little black eyes and a flat orange beak. It cocked its little head and looked at me.

"You know how to take care of him now. See that you do," my uncle said as he stepped back from the car.

My parents were too surprised to say anything, I think. I smiled at my uncle and thanked him. Then we all waved goodbye as we left. On the way home I thought of the perfect name for my duck. I called him 'Jeremiah Kincaid Donald McQuack,'

I didn't have Jeremiah very long. My father built a cage for him in the garden in a spot where I had had a sandbox when I was little. The sandbox was the place where I first sampled insect cuisine. My mother found me eating caterpillars there once. At any rate, I hadn't played there for a while and so my father thought it would be a good spot for my new pet.

Jeremiah stayed in his pen except when I was around outside, which was most of the day that summer, and then he followed me around the yard, quacking and investigating things all around me. He was very good at finding insects and frogs and other little critters and that fascinated me. In the autumn I went off to school and so he was penned up most of the day. I didn't think about his imprisonment much. I would let him out as soon as I got home. He was a big duck by this time. I thought he was so pretty with his blue feathers around his neck and his light orange bill.

I remember that one time after the first frost, I let him out after school before I went in to change clothes. I had on my new light beige, school coat. I let Jeremiah run around the yard by the persimmon tree, and he was busy picking up and devouring the ripe persimmons. After a bit I decided that I should catch him and pick him up to put him back in his pen so I could go in the house to change…and when I picked him up, he smeared persimmon muck all over my coat. I didn't notice the coat, but I thought it was funny that he got the muck in my hair and on my face…however, my mother wasn't pleased when she saw the coat!

Soon after that my father announced that he had found a winter home for Jeremiah. A farmer who had ducks and a pond was willing to take him. Supposedly it was just for the winter. I was very anxious because, as my brother pointed out, it was just before Thanksgiving, and some people enjoyed eating duck for their holiday meal. My father assured me that Jeremiah was not to be a meal. He was just going to be with some other ducks on a pond on a farm. I really had no choice.

Later, when I asked if we could go visit him, my father said he would talk to the farmer, and then he reported back to me that Jeremiah had flown off south with some other ducks that had rested for a night on the pond. I was suspicious, but my father pointed out that Jeremiah was a mallard. He had those blue feathers like the wild mallards and so he probably just fit in with them. I could tell that my brother didn't believe this story either, but I pretended that I did believe, and my brother never told me his actual thoughts on the subject. I was rather hesitant to eat duck after that, though.

******

And so again I return to think about Rapunzel as I swim. The story has a tower, long hair, briars, betrayal of trust, keeping of promises, adoption, married love, the valuing of the married partner over the child, exotic food, the tendency of the child to believe what he or she is told, or to interpret what he or she sees according to what has been told by adults …so many things.

And who is the villain? We are led to believe that it is the witch next door. The witch with the big, alluring, garden. But we never learn just why the witch wants a child, and why does she want to keep the child in a tower? And what if the child had been a boy? Or was it all witchcraft and the mother who pined for rampion just a vessel for a preordained pregnancy? I suppose there could be variants of the story that weave these possibilities into the story, but my version did not address these thoughts. In the version I read, the reader is just expected to believe that the witch wanted a child to keep isolated in a tower. Indeed it makes me wonder if that witch might have been an early Miss Haversham, from Dickens' novel, and Rapunzel was supposed to be Estella.

Oh, the things we can learn from our wandering thoughts. There are people everywhere who live disappointed lives and act on their disappointments in ways that are not entirely acceptable, or may seem acceptable but are detrimental to someone else...

Once, my family went with a group of boating people for a weekend at Big Bone Island. I loved that island. I believe that it has since vanished beneath the Ohio because of a huge dam that was constructed sometime after the events of this story occurred. At any rate, we were at Big Bone and, as usual, I was in the water, swimming and frolicking with the other children. My parents had discovered that they needed to go to a town that was located downstream a few miles and as that meant they would need to be gone for several hours, they had called to me and told me that I needed to go with them.

I was so disappointed! I argued about going with them. I pointed out that there were many people that we knew that were watching their children play in the water, and perhaps those people could watch me, too. I must have made my case pretty well, because my parents decided that I could stay and that a couple from my hometown...good friends of ours...could watch out for me at the same time that they watched out for their own children. I was told that if they told me to get out of the water, I was to get out. I agreed. I felt that agreeing to that in itself was a rather great concession as this particular couple was pretty over-protective of their children. At least that is what I thought. I knew that their boys had to rest after eating, and they could only be in the sun for a certain, well-monitored time and that they had to wear hats and, well, today they would be seen as practicing necessary caution, but then, they seemed overly careful of their boys.

I had known them my whole life. The older boy was my brother's age and the younger boy was my age. Both boys were a little different from other children that I knew. The younger boy, my friend, had been born with a disfiguring mark on the side of his face, and he was also a little awkwardly shaped with a rather large head for his body build. The older boy was rather fragile looking. He was very thin, and he had a very thin, narrow face. They looked very different from one another. Neither boy was athletic.

I had always enjoyed playing with the younger boy, because we had some interests in common. He was interested in world events such as the coronation of Queen Elizabeth II. He even liked to act events like that out, and so did I. His parents had let him have puppets and dolls, which was

138

unusual behavior for the parents of boys at that time, and he liked to play with my dolls, too. He and I would set up elaborate scenes of the coronation, or of operas, or of fairytales and such.

And so it happened that my parents, as well as my brother who wanted to go with them, left Big Bone, waving to me as I stood in the water, waving good-bye to them.

Now it is important that you know about that island. I don't know just how it got its name. I always imagined that a dinosaur bone had been discovered there, and I had dug around quite a bit, hoping to find another bone. The water of the Ohio was split as it encountered the island and there was a deep channel where the large boats such as the barges with their towboats or the Delta Queen could travel safely, and then on the other side of the island was a more narrow channel which was deep enough for the smaller pleasure craft, but neither wide enough nor deep enough for the barges. As the water joined together on the downstream side of the island it left a long pointed sandbar, wide where it was closest to the island and gradually growing more narrow and coming to a point further out from the island. At the very furthest point of the sandbar, far out from the island itself, a thick branch emerged from deep beneath the water. It might have been more than a branch at one time. Perhaps, before any of the dams were on the river, it had been a tree, and now, as it was mostly covered with water, it had become a drowned tree. It was lifeless, but still must have had deep roots that held on to the river bottom against the merging currants from the two sides of the island.

On the day I am describing, I was playing close to the island on the sandbar under the water. There were younger children sitting on the beach, digging little lakes and filling them with water from the river, and there were slightly older children chasing each other around, playing ball with a beach ball and cheerfully falling into the water as they wished. It was in this atmosphere that some of the oldest children, including my temporary 'guardians'' oldest son, suggested that we play 'follow the leader'. I was last in line, because I had been watching my family leave, but I didn't mind. It was a long line of children, and we walked back and forth, hopping, jumping, falling…copying the leader's movements. Several people took turns and then my friend's older brother took his turn. There was some whispering among those at the front, and then he began leading everyone out into the deeper water.

I was still at the very end of the line, but even I began to sense that we were venturing out a bit too far. At first we were nearly in line with the dead tree that marked the end of the sandbar, but I noticed that we seemed to be going a bit to one side. I was fairly short at the time and the water was getting deeper and deeper for me.

Suddenly the line stopped, and there was laughter coming from the front of the line. They were calling my name! "It's your turn to be leader!" they all called.

I moved out of line toward the center of the sandbar and said, "Okay! Everyone follow me!" And I started to turn around to lead everyone back in to the island.

"No! You have to come to the front of the line!" they called. Everyone started to laugh again, because it was obvious that I was too short to go out where the oldest boys were standing with just their heads above the water!

"I can't do that!" I retorted, trying to stay good natured about the joke on me. "You guys have just got to follow me back in!" I stepped back into the wavering line of laughing children, and as I did so I felt the sand beneath my feet slipping away, and I felt the current of the river around my ankles suddenly increase in strength. I automatically flopped over on my belly and began to swim with my strongest stroke, the breaststroke, toward the island.

I didn't see what had happened behind me. I assumed that they were all behind me, either following 'the leader', or just coming back in to the more shallow water, now that they had played their joke. I finally lifted my head to see how close I was to the island and reached down with my feet to find the familiar sand. As I stood up, I remember that I was laughing…intentionally, to show that I wasn't mad or embarrassed about the joke that they had pulled on me…but I saw that the little children on the beach were staring beyond me at something. I stopped and turned around to see that no one from the entire line of children was behind me. Instead, they were floating away down the river. Some of them, those that had on lifejackets, were waving and calling for help. The others were thrashing and screaming, trying to keep their heads above water, and the river was carrying them unrelentingly away. Around the downstream bend came a long, loud blast from the towboat of a barge and the very front of the big flat prow of a loaded barge was just coming into view. That explained the sudden increase of current. The barges, with their powerful engines sucked at the river water and created what was called the undertow, a name I suddenly understood.

I turned to the little children up on the beach and yelled, "Go get a grown-up! Go get help!" I was struggling against the undertow that was pulling hard on my ankles and legs, and I could barely walk through the water, let alone run, even though it was less than knee-deep . The little children just stood staring as if transfixed. I bellowed again, "Go! Go and get a grown-up!"

Finally one child turned and bolted up the hill to where all the grown-ups must have retreated for some reason. By that time, I was up on the beach and panting and running as fast as I could. I raced up the hill and into a circle of grown-ups who were building a campfire, visiting and enjoying what was probably lukewarm beer.

"A bunch of the kids are floating down the river, and there is a barge coming!" I gasped.

No one moved.

I was stunned. I tried again, "They are going to drown if you can't get to them!"

The little boy who had gotten there first said, "It's what I said was happening!"

One man looked around at the others and said, "I think we'd better look. I don't think they'd both lie!" And he got up and hopped over to the top of the path to get a look, turned back with a look of panic on his face and said, "We've got to get the boats out there and fast!"

From then on, it was chaotic as various men ran to loosen their boats and grab life jackets and poles to help grab the children. I watched as one-by-one the drifting, struggling children were rescued. One child had gone under completely and an adult had had to dive in to get him. Another child had managed to grab a branch on the dead tree and held on until the others were scooped up to safety, and then he was rescued. The barge had blown another warning blast and her men were lining the sides of the craft, and, I think, the pilot had cut her speed. On the island we knew when the last child close to the barge had been rescued because the bargemen cheered and waved to us! We, on the shore, all sighed in relief.

I stood on the sidelines as the sobbing, hysterical children were carried ashore and reunited with their parents. My parents' friends were among the relieved adults. There was a general commotion as everyone tried to find out just what had happened. We all gravitated up the hill from the beach so that the traumatized children could be warmed up by the fire. I was on the outside of all this, because I hadn't been in danger, and because my parents weren't there.

The children were trying to tell how they had stepped off the sandbar, or were swept off the sandbar and the parents were trying to understand. Finally some child said, "We were playing 'Follow the leader'! And we went out too far!"

One of the parents said, in that voice that a frightened and now recovering parent uses when they want to impress their beloved child, "You are just lucky that we were told what was happening!"

And for a moment, a thought crossed my mind…I was a hero of a sort. I was the one who had gotten the help. I had even gotten the little boy to go first…but no one had lis…

And then, at that moment, my parents' friend asked, "Who was the leader?"

And my friend's brother, the one who had led us all out so far in order to embarrass me about my height, said my name.

Everything changed for me with lightening speed. My mother's friend grabbed me and threw me to the ground. She pummeled me with her fists, and then she began kicking me with all the rage that a person can have when they feel that they might have lost everything that was most important to them.

Someone, I think the man who had told his child how lucky he had been to be rescued, pulled the half, or fully-crazed, woman off of me, and I used that moment to run blindly into the thick brush of the island.

I think I remember someone calling after me, but I am not certain. I ran deeper and deeper into the island. None of us had ever ventured very far into the island because it was covered with brambles and thick underbrush. I don't remember seeing anything but river willow saplings and weeds. The briars tangled around my bare legs and tore my bathing suit. I was caked with mud and bloodstained by the time I slowed down and realized that I couldn't hear anything anymore except the dull drone of cicadas and the rustle of the weeds as they were disturbed by the small birds whose solitary lives I had invaded.

Finally, exhausted, I crouched down in the sandy mud among the reeds and willows and brambles, and I rested. My mind was numb. I crouched there the rest of the day. I watched as the shadows grew longer and the daytime insects began to quiet and the evening chorus of frogs and crickets began to sound. I watched the sky darken and the first stars emerge, cold and blinking down at me. I heard an owl and a solitary cry of a different night bird. I must have been cold, but I was too numb to notice. At last I heard a voice calling me. I didn't answer at first. The call came closer, and I knew it was my father. The evening creatures became very still, and I heard him call again. I began to cry, and he heard me. He parted the weeds and gathered me up. He carried me out from the center of the island and down the steep slope to the water's edge. He had moved our boat away from the others and moored it here. He lifted me up and into the boat. My mother and brother were there. My mother washed me up and cleaned my scratches. She took off my tattered bathing suit and wrapped me in a towel. No one ever mentioned the whole incident again.

And the backstory? I'm not certain but I have gathered a few bits of information that may explain some of the events...but, as when I am presented with facts that are supposed to debunk some of my most dearly held superstitious beliefs...I'm not sure which way to go. Or maybe I am just reluctant to embrace these bits.

My mother's friend, Joan, had been married longer than my mother and was a few years older when they met. Joan and her husband had been trying to have a child, but she had suffered miscarriage after miscarriage. When Joan had announced that she was finally pregnant, and it seemed to be 'taking', my mother, newer to the community, perhaps unaware of the trauma that had gone before for Joan, or, perhaps, simply caught up with her own good news, had happily announced her own news that she too was expecting. This didn't happen just one unlucky time. It happened twice. The first time my mother gave birth to a robust, red-headed boy, my brother, and Joan produced a thin, rather sickly, frail boy. The second time my mother produced a girl. No matter that I was rather wiry and covered with eczema, I was a girl which did follow the revered 'boy first, girl second' pattern, and Joan gave birth to my playmate, a boy with a disfiguring mark on his face. Because Joan had had so many miscarriages, people whispered behind her back that her children were misbegotten and probably should not have survived. It had even been suspected that both boys might be feeble-minded, but this was certainly not so. They may have been rather unusual boys, but they were both certainly bright, and the younger child turned out to be extremely talented artistically. At any rate, it may be that my mother had accidently sparked a jealousy by bearing children that seemed more acceptable to the community…or it may be that Joan had suffered so for her children that the thought that she had almost lost them both because of my supposed leadership in that wretched game just caused her to snap. I can only guess about this now. But even knowing this tiny bit helps me to hold the pain at a distance.

And how does this relate to 'Rapunzel' and the world of fairytale? The witch? Perhaps. I sense the jealousy of the witch. And I certainly felt the violence of a witch-like fury, the fury of my mother's friend when she thought I had nearly deprived her of her hard won children. That fury is somehow similar in my mind to the rage of the witch when she felt she was losing what she thought should have been her possession.

I am swimming again. Back and forth. I have the pool to myself. Why do I think of Rapunzel when I swim? Rapunzel surely never went swimming. All that hair! It would have tangled around her. If she wore a bathing cap (do they even sell those anymore?) It would have made her head like a lead weight, and she would have been an upside down 'Weeble' on the bottom of the lake. Poor Rapunzel! I'm sure that she missed the pleasure of feeling the water move against her body, and the satisfaction of gliding across the surface, barely making a ripple as she went. When I curl my body up and slowly roll over in the water, I look up at the bottom sides of the birds that fly far above me, dark silhouettes against the blue sky that seems to go up forever. Poor Rapunzel! I float, motionless, and watch a large hawk coasting, then adjusting his wings as he goes into a curve above me, and then a single stroke, and he coasts again, making minor adjustments as he moves away.

Once, when my daughter was fifteen, she and I went to visit my oldest son and his wife and their newborn child. I was trying to be helpful. I was folding laundry and washing dishes and tidying up, and my daughter was holding the baby and visiting with my daughter-in-law. During a lull in the conversation, I reminded my daughter that we had with us the materials for a project she had been planning to do for a contest. She had taken a photo of a girlfriend when they had been swimming. When my daughter's friend had come to the surface after diving into the pool, her hair extensions had floated out, encircling her face. The photo was stunning. For the contest my daughter was to write a little journalistic story that would accompany a photo and then mount both story and photo on a poster board and submit it for judging.

My daughter had the photo, the poster board, and all the materials for putting it together, but she hadn't finished writing the story. All she needed to do was to finish writing it and, then, print it out and put everything together. The deadline for entering was the next day, and I reminded her that if she would take a few minutes to finish, she would be free to hold the baby and visit the rest of the day.

She groaned and rolled her eyes and looked at her sister-in-law for help. She whined. She pouted. I knew that I was coming off as the wicked witch who puts a damper on everything. It was rapidly turning into a power struggle. I finally said, "Oh, throw a tantrum. I don't care! You need to finish this project. You have everything you need to finish it. You have done most of the work. Even if you don't turn it in for the contest, you should finish it by the deadline just to teach yourself how to do things for a deadline." And I left the room in a huff.

She finished it. She put it together, and it looked great. My daughter-in-law made a fuss over the finished project. We enjoyed the rest of the visit.

To make a long story a tiny bit shorter, we delivered the finished poster to be judged, and it won first place. Then it went to a higher level in the contest, and it won first place there. Finally, it went to the highest level of the contest, and for that level, my daughter had to travel clear across the state and stay overnight with a family she didn't know and then, on the next day, she was to be interviewed about her work on the poster by the judge.

The day before the interview, we drove her to stay with the host family and then agreed to meet her after her interview in order to wait for the announcement of the winner of the contest. She wasn't nervous, she said. She knew there was a lot of competition, and she thought that the 'host family stay' would be her prize!

When we met her the next day, she said that she had had a good time with her host family. They were Jewish, and she was able to learn about the Jewish Sabbath firsthand. It had been a wonderful experience. The interview had been more of a trial. The original judge for the contest had gotten sick and had cancelled and so there had been a last minute change of judges. The new judge had been a man from a large urban newspaper whose background was photojournalism—a professional journalist, not a teacher who was used to dealing with young teenagers!

We waited with her and visited with her host family. Finally we were all taken into a large auditorium for the contest results. After a few speeches they announced the winners in the usual fashion of third place, second place, first place and then, Grand Champion. The Grand Champion prize was an all expense paid, ten-day trip to visit Israel. My daughter won it.

We were dumbfounded to say the least. The woman from my daughter's host family took my hand, beamed at me, and said, "I knew it! I knew our girl would win the trip!" And everyone stood up and clapped as our completely stunned daughter walked to the stage as the Grand Champion winner.

After the ceremony, and after the meeting with the coordinators of the trip where all the details were explained, in a quiet moment just after we silently, still stunned, had walked to the car, my daughter turned to me, took my arm to turn me so she could look into my eyes, and she said, "Thank you." We both knew why.

When she returned from Israel, she was full of stories about the sights and experiences she had had. She had taken photos of all the special places she had visited, and she had taken photos of many 'cute boys'. She had an assortment of gifts for us and mementoes for herself. For me she had a special gift. It was a rather bedraggled looking plastic bottle filled with mud and water. She said, "I was swimming in the Dead Sea, and everyone around me was laughing at how buoyant you feel in that water...and I thought of you! I thought, 'if my mother were here, she would be floating six inches above this water', so I brought some of it back for you along with some of the salty mud."

Maybe Rapunzel, even with all that hair, would float in the Dead Sea.

******

'Look me in the eye'. I've heard that saying all the years of my life. I learned as a little child that when a person wanted to be certain that you understood what they were saying to you, that they would use that little phrase. I learned, too, that if you didn't look someone 'in the eye', that they would think that you were lying. But sometimes looking others 'in the eye' is difficult. Sometimes peoples' eyes are scary. Crazed. For years I could not look people in the eye without a feeling of panic. I would have to swallow a terrible fear in order to look into the eyes of others.

For the most part, people assumed that I was shy when they noticed that I had a hard time looking directly at them. For the most part they did not think that I was lying. And, most often, I was not lying, although, I admit, I'm sure I had my share of evasive moments! But I digress. There is a story behind my fear of looking into eyes, also.

When I was about seven, my mother thought that it would be nice for us to go together on a hike in the woods and look for wildflowers. It must have been early spring although I am no longer certain. My mother loved flowers, and she had filled our garden with many varieties. She had 'domesticated flowers' planted so that there was something blooming in every season, from crocus and tulip and hyacinth in the spring, to, in summer, iris and peonies, then poppies and roses and daisies, and marigolds. In the autumn we were surrounded by chrysanthemums, and in winter our rooms were crowded with all manner of blooming house plants such as violets and forced bulbs like amaryllis and narcissus. But, at that time, many people nourished flower gardens where we lived, so she was not so very unique.

However, she did have a special interest that I never saw in anyone else's garden. She had a wildflower garden. She had chosen a spot close to an old apple tree where there was both light and shade, and she had gathered plants from the woods around us to plant there. She had Trillium, Jack-in-the–Pulpit, Spring Beauty, May apple, Bloodroot, Dutch-man's Britches, and so many others. She told me stories about these plants, too. Some were poisonous if you ate them. Some were thought to cure illnesses. Some, simply, had stories associated with them. I think she had learned about these plants from her great-aunts, or perhaps her grandmother. But some of the stories were from her reading, because she loved to read. At any rate, we were to go to the woods to look for wildflowers.

We had dressed in our hiking clothes. We had a wildflower guide book with us and a canteen of water, in case we got thirsty. We drove the short distance to the woods where my mother wanted to go. That in itself was an adventure, because my mother had just recently gotten her driving license. I think she may have had one before she had gotten married, but she had never owned a car, so she had not had much experience with driving. She had been in a car accident once as a passenger, and she was a little shy about being the driver and, therefore, responsible if there were an accident. Anyway, we drove to the edge of the woods.

The first part of the hike was a delight. It was a beautiful warm day, and the cool woods enveloped us. We wandered about among the trees, focusing on the plants that grew among the leaf litter that coated the ground. My mother told me the names of the various flowering plants and then she showed me some things about plants to help me recognize them when they weren't in flower. She showed me how on some plants the leaves were arranged one way and on some others, they were arranged differently. She showed me how some leaves had veins that made one type of pattern and on others another type of pattern. She didn't have terms for these differences, so the only way she could describe them to me was to show me…and have me show her what I noticed. It was a treasure hunt and my mother was full of thoughts and stories about the plants we were finding. I remember that she told me a story about an Indian boy who had been captured by white soldiers and, as he was marched along a wooded path back to the white settlement, he vowed to fall upon a May apple plant and eat it, thus poisoning himself, but, she assured me, something stopped him and the story ended well.

We walked quietly among the trees, listening to the birds and pausing to follow each rustle among the leaves with our eyes. There were so many little quiet sounds that revealed the life of the world of the woods. I never, in my life, ran and shouted in the woods the way some people do, because my mother had taught me that the woodland is the home of other creatures who depend on the quiet to keep themselves safe and content. We were so engrossed in our discoveries that day, and in the stories that my mother told, that the afternoon began to slip away from us.

We came to a fence, and that fence perplexed my mother. She decided that we should climb it as it was beginning to get late. We needed to head home, and crossing the fence would get us back to the car a little faster. After climbing the fence, as we moved down a slope through the thinning woodland, my mother spotted some cattle. She seemed uncomfortable about being on the same side of the fence with them. I wasn't certain just why she was uncomfortable, because I thought that cattle were pretty tame animals. I knew nothing about bulls. All cattle were cows to me at that time.

My mother was keeping an eye on the cattle when I broke one of the cardinal rules of hiking. I had moved ahead of her a bit, looking for better footing on the cattle-worn slope, and I moved back a thorn covered branch that was in my way, and then I released it. The branch slapped back into my mother's face. I heard a gasp and an anguished cry. I turned to see my mother, frozen in an attitude of pain, her hands covering her eye. She was gasping as though she couldn't get her breath. I began asking "What's wrong! What's wrong!"

"There is something in my eye," she gasped, obviously trying to control both her pain and her panic. Then she added, between measured breaths, "You will have to look at it."

I don't know what I expected to see, but I will never forget what I saw. She moved her hands away from her face slowly. Her face was rigid with the pain. In her eye, right in the center of her pupil, was a thorn.

"Tell me what you see," she said in a low controlled voice, as though I were looking at a rare bird through the only binoculars we had.

I tried to imitate her tone and control, though my heart and mind were racing away from me. "I see a thorn sticking out of your eye," I said in a low voice. I heard myself. My voice wasn't shaking.

We stood like that for a few minutes. My mother's face was covered with tears and some dirt. The tears were dripping from her cheek and chin. I said nothing. She was waiting for some terrible pain to stop, I could tell.

"Is that blood on my face?" she asked.

"No. No blood, just tears," I answered.

"Good," my mother replied. Then she added, "Where are the cattle?"

I looked on down the slope at the cattle, nonchalantly grazing and moving, step-by-step, further away from us. They seemed so peaceful and distant. I felt my heart slowing down.

"They are just eating grass and moving away from us," I said.

"Good," my mother said. We stood there a few more minutes. Then my mother said, "I can't close my eye. It is too painful. You will have to pull the thorn out."

"I can't," I gasped, horror stricken.

My mother said, "You have to. I can't think of any way around it. Every time I blink, the thorn is going in further and it hurts more and more." And then she added, "And after you take out the thorn, you will have to lead me home."

"Lead you home?" I repeated incredulously.

"Yes," my mother answered. Her breathing was still ragged as with pain. "I can't see."

"But," I started.

"I can't see out of either eye," she said, and I could hear the panic entering her voice.

My mind was racing again. I couldn't gather my thoughts; they were scattering all through the woods, hiding under the leaves, climbing the trees, burrowing into the ground.

"Okay," I heard myself say. "But my hands are dirty. I'd better use the water to wash them off a bit." I couldn't believe I was saying that. I couldn't believe that I was thinking that.

"Good." My mother said.

I took the canteen of water and opened it with shaking hands. I spilled the water over my right hand and then looked for a place to dry it. My clothes were all dirty. I used my left hand to pull out my undershirt from under my blouse. It looked clean. I dried my right hand on it.

I told my mother that I had washed my hands, and that I was ready to take the thorn out.

She was silent. I could hear her breathing. She was holding her head in a stiff and unnatural position. I looked around to try to find the best place to stand. I got as close to her as I could, and I held onto her arm.

"Mommy, I can't reach your eye," I finally had to say.

"Oh, yes, of course. Keep holding on to me so I don't fall, and I will squat down a little. I can't move my head because I think that moving it moves the thorn."

Some part of me felt that we were working together, and I only had to do my part. I steadied her as she began to squat down. "There," I said. She held her position, and I took a deep breath.

I looked her in the eye.

I carefully moved my right hand up to her watering eye and, as gently as I could, I grasped the thorn with my small fingers and pulled it out. Clear liquid streamed from the wound. No blood.

"There," I said. "It is out." But my mother knew. I felt her rigid muscles relax a bit. The pain was abating some. She straightened up, still holding her head in that awkward way.

"What did it look like?" she asked.

"Tears came out of the hole when I took the thorn out," I said.

"Clear? That was something called the lens, I think. I've read about it somewhere."

"I thought it would be blood, but it wasn't," I said.

"I'm better," my mother said. "I can't see though. You have to lead me down the hill. Look for the gate. Be sure I know where to step, I mustn't fall down now."

I led her, step-by-step, down the slope. The cattle were far away from us now, and I told my mother that. I kept up a chatter about the slope and where she should put her feet, and she held onto me with an iron grasp as she slowly followed me down to the level field and then on toward the gate.

"What about the car?" I asked.

"We will just have to leave it. Daddy can get it later. Just lead me up toward town. Maybe you will see someone to stop that can give us a ride to Doctor Lewis' house."

And so we made our slow way toward the town. We had just reached the outmost part of the town where there were sidewalks, when a car pulled over and someone I didn't know called over, "Peg? What's wrong?" and then they got out and hurried my mother into their car and hurried me into the backseat. They took my mother to Doc Lewis' office, and I sat in the familiar old waiting room steeped in the smell of antiseptic. My father came rushing in and hurried into the room where Doc Lewis had taken my mother.

Later I remember being home. Someone must have taken me there. A multitude of people, friends of my parents, came and had made up a bed for my mother in our living room. I remember being alone on the far side of that room with a crowd of people standing by my mother. I couldn't get close to her. There were too many people, big people, and I could only see their backs and hear their muted talk. It seemed to me that my mother was so far away and so many things were between us, that even though I could see out of both of my eyes, I couldn't see her.

******

Look into my eyes. One restless night, as a middle-aged woman, I had a dream. It was a long and complicated drama as often my dreams are. Somehow I was in a city which was under siege, and I was alone with my children, seven children I think, and they were all young again. We were with a group of rebel fighters who were trying to help us escape. Everything was orange and glowing with fire, and the air was filled with gun shots and the whistling of bombs. The men spoke a different language from me. I understood that they were trying to help me, but I was not sure what I needed to do.

The men brought large wicker baskets into the tower room where I was hiding. They motioned that they were going to put my children into the baskets and then they would carry them to a safe place. I remember that the gunshots sounded closer and closer. I could see flames outside the tower window. I was so very frightened. I could not understand how my children would fit into those baskets, however. Surely there was a better plan!

One of the men, a muscular man with a swarthy unfamiliar face, but with eyes that were somehow familiar, looked into my eyes and then showed me some liquid he had in a bottle. He indicated that he was going to give it to my children.

"No!" I cried. "Please don't poison them!" I was shocked and frightened. He looked at me, his familiar eyes were pleading with me to understand. I hesitated. The room was filling with smoke, and the papers on one side of the tower room were beginning to curl up from the heat. Fearfully and reluctantly, I nodded assent and watched as he quickly administered the liquid, a spoonful to each small trusting, child. I watched as his men then somehow folded my children gently, and placed them, one at a time, into each of the baskets.

One-by-one, the men shouldered the baskets and hurried down the spiral tower stairs. The swarthy man motioned for me to follow them all as he took up his weapon and covered our escape from behind me.

We wound through the smoky, flaming city streets, avoiding the fallen rubble and dodging behind crumbling walls. I held a shawl over my head and used it to cover my mouth and nose against the smoke and debris in the air. I had lost all sense of direction. I had no idea where we might be headed. I thought that perhaps we were trying to get to the river and away from the fire.

Suddenly the line of basket-carrying men stopped. The man before me motioned for me to be silent. A few minutes later we moved forward with much more caution. The swarthy man patted my shoulder as he moved past me and up to the front of the line. A few minutes later I could see that, one at a time, the basket carriers were lowering themselves into what looked to be a sewer opening. When it was my turn, the swarthy man helped me into the black, dank hole.

Everyone was silent. There was a scraping sound as the swarthy man pulled the sewer lid shut above his head. I heard his shoes as he dropped down to the damp floor where the rest of us waited in the dark. There was some rustling and then the flare of a torch.

I could see, for an instant, the black walls and low, dripping ceiling. The swarthy man motioned the basket carriers to follow as he gave the lead man the torch, and we set out again at a slower pace.

I could see nothing, and my footing was so very unsure, that, after a few moments, the swarthy man came up behind me and gently nudged me forward. He felt for my arm and then took my hand and shoved it up to grip the leather strap of the basket that was being carried in front of me. Then he fell back from me.

The dark was such that there was nothing for my eyes to adjust to. I slipped and stumbled along, hanging onto the strap. My body was bruised from hitting the wall as we twisted and turned along some corridor or another under the city. The reek of the stagnant water that we were wading through was mixed with the stench of the sewer that must have been running close by. I held on.

There was a reverberating sound of gunfire in the dark that echoed in my ears. The swarthy man came from behind and pushed me down just as the basket carrier before me began to crouch. The darkness of the tunnel lit up in flashes as there was an exchange of fire. Bullets were ricocheting from the stone walls. Then it was silent again except for the sound of dripping. No one spoke as I heard the carriers cautiously moving to stand again. I heard something being dragged aside and then, a quiet splash as if something had been nudged into a stream of water. The swarthy man returned with the torch, and he shown it in my face and looked over my body. His eyes were questioning. I tried to smile to let him know that I was all right. He nodded and glanced behind me into the dark. Then he turned and headed toward the front of the line.

Now we traveled faster. Someone knew where we were and had tried to ambush us. We twisted and turned so that it reminded me of being the tail in the children's game of 'crack the whip'. And then my thoughts turned back to my children, folded into those baskets, jostled and shaken. And, as we turned again in the dark and tried to shuffle quietly through the unrelenting water, slipping and straining to stay on our feet, I thought about the bullets, the ricocheting bullets.

My breath caught in my throat. Any one of those bullets might have hit a basket. My child, anyone of my children, might now be silently bleeding away to death. Or they might already to be dead. I pictured in my mind, my folded children bloody and lifeless, their beautiful smiling eyes glassy and vacant…

We turned abruptly to go a different direction, and I thought to myself, "Let go! No one would ever find you here in this maze! You could drown or starve and rot in this stinking place and no one would…"

And the swarthy man, as if summoned by something; a thought, a dream, a whisper; pushed back along the line of carriers and pulled my face up and looked me in the eye. I hesitated and smiled through the tears that were streaming down my face.

He moved again to the front. We continued. The dark was becoming stifling. We must have been approaching Hell itself. The stench was stronger and more raw. Again we turned and this time, I slipped and fell. As the carrier before me paused to let me catch a grip on the strap again, I felt something warm and damp dripping from the basket he was shouldering. Again I saw in my mind the blood of my children. And again, as if summoned by my despair, the swarthy man paused the line and returned to me to make me look into his eyes as he looked into mine. Once more, I nodded as I regained my resolve.

The third time that I despaired, I tightened my grip on the strap that held me to the path, and I closed my eyes and conjured all the strength and power of his eyes, of his look. And I pushed the fear out of me.

The air began to freshen. The tunnel became less dark. As I opened my eyes, I began to make out shapes before me, and then the carriers before me were silhouetted against a dark grey, star-studded sky. All was silence. One-by-one, the carriers loaded their baskets into waiting rowboats and then they, themselves, boarded. The swarthy man and I were settled into the last boat. I was lain face up in the bow and lightly covered with blankets. Again the swarthy man looked at me and his eyes seemed to say "rest, we are almost there."

I watched the stars. I heard the water rushing beneath the hull as I rested. I felt the boat's bow, so close to me, as it rhythmically, split through the water with each pull of the oars. I heard the soft noise as those oars entered the water and rose from it, and I heard the low sound of the man whose straining muscles were moving me slowly to safety.

At last we abruptly bumped into the shore on the other side. I must have been asleep because, as I opened my eyes, I saw that it was almost dawn. The first streaks of light and color were creeping above the land in the east. I was gently, carefully helped out of the rocking, wavering boat, and I stood a minute, steadying my legs after the terrible journey through the city and tunnel and across the water. I watched the carriers as they carefully handed out the baskets which held my children.

Again the dread and fear began to creep up into my head from my belly. I staggered and turned to follow the carriers as they silently moved up the slope from the shore toward a small lighted building.

As we entered the building, there were hugs and handshakes and slapping of backs all in a language I didn't understand. And then there was an almost reverential silence as they saw me.

The swarthy man said something and the carriers turned to the baskets. I couldn't look. I turned away. My eyes couldn't stand to see them, my babies, my children, bloody and dead of either bullets or poison.

There was an audible sigh, and I turned my face again toward the baskets in time to see my children, lifted out, one at a time, and then, slowly unfolding themselves, stretching and yawning and smiling.

I woke from this dream, amazed. I ran into my bathroom to wash my face and wake myself. I looked up into my bathroom mirror, water still dripping from my face, and, I saw those somehow familiar eyes. The swarthy man's eyes. My eyes. Look into my eyes. Don't let go.

My own eyes.

******

As an adult, I took my own children out into the woods. I tried to teach them those things about the plants and creatures and life of the woodland that my mother had taught me. And I also tried to teach them about branches and thorns and stepping carefully.

Sometimes, early in the morning, there is fog held captive in the low-lying areas along creeks and ponds. I remember walking through those swirling mists holding my daughter's hand. The fog was so thick that we could not see each other, although we were close together, but we knew where we both were, because we held hands.

Hands. There is another Grimm's story about a girl who loses her hands. I went to a lecture once that was given by a published poet, a man of letters, and he was excited about fairy tales that spoke to young men. Someone in the audience asked if he knew of any particularly 'good' fairy tales that would speak to the empowering of young women. The poet was not pleased with this question, because he was only interested in restoring the power of young men, but he paused a moment and said, "Some think that Grimm's story of 'The Girl With No Hands' is empowering for women." Then he resumed his talk.

I was interested in this because I had never noticed this story much. It had not seemed empowering to me! A girl is sold to the devil by her father who has been tricked into this bargain. She cleverly eludes that fate but then her father chops off her hands because of his fear of the devil! Her father offers to care for her, but she goes out on her own, has many adventures and hardships, eventually meets a man who loves her and has artificial hands made for her, but then, he, too, is tricked by the devil. Finally she goes off by herself and God gives her back her real hands, because of her 'piety'. It ends with a tearful reuniting of the girl and her husband. Yuck.

This story angered me. I began to look for variants and soon found an African story that followed a similar path. In this version the girl is betrayed, also. A dearly loved male family member chops off her hand because of greed. The girl wanders, falls in love, is betrayed again and finally when she thinks all hope is gone, tries one last desperate thing to try to rescue her child who is in peril, and magically, both of her hands are there, and she is able to save the child.

The key difference between the two versions seems to me to be the way the girl gets back her hands. In the African version the girl gets her hands back by overcoming her own feelings of helplessness. At the moment of crisis, a snake(!) that she has saved through her general kindness, says to her, basically, "Try! You might not succeed because you are crippled and society says you are worthless, but try anyway!" Her hands are suddenly there when she needs them-- because she conquers her own fears and tries to do something in spite of what she has been told about herself, not because she was a good girl that God rewarded for piety! For me, that is empowering.

Back to Rapunzel. Rapunzel is betrayed in a different way, first by her father who 'gives' her away to the witch (in some versions he tells his wife that the baby has died), and then by the young man who, in some versions, woos her into letting down her hair and then seduces her. Rapunzel has no way of knowing about men, sex, pregnancy…but the young man knows about these things!

It is possible for a young woman, especially a sheltered young woman, to be ignorant about sex. Today it wouldn't be easy, but I think it might be possible still for a girl to be almost 'blinded' to the realities of her body. Literature is full of stories about girls who have been kept in ignorance, and, indeed, what adult woman hasn't known of a girl who had no idea that she might begin bleeding between her legs and that this was normal? Our culture, and many cultures around the world, have conspired to keep girls ignorant. Girls in touch with nature, of course, could observe sex, and birth and death, but often it was thought to be inappropriate for a girl to observe such things…and the result was that many girls have matured without knowing much about sex or themselves! Usually girls haven't been kept in towers, however.

My father's oldest sister was born in 1908. She married her high school beau after finishing high school, attending college, and teaching school for several years. She did not date other men often, although she did date others occasionally, especially in college. However when she married, she was shocked to learn what was expected to happen between her husband and herself on the wedding night. She was so shocked that she locked herself in the bathroom and the young husband had to call her parents and explain the situation. I remember this story about my aunt. I heard it first as a young, married woman. I found it hard to believe, however.

When my aunt was in her 90's, she was moved by her son into a retirement center, and I went to visit her there. We had had some comfortable history together, as I had stayed with her as a young girl, and she and I had had some funny experiences together. At any rate, I had always been curious about this odd story, but I had never thought to ask her about it…too personal and, perhaps, embarrassing.

Somehow, this visit was different. She had lived alone for quite a long time, with only her little dog as a companion, and now she was in a 'home', no matter how independent she still felt. Her neighbors in her new residence were dying at a little too frequent a pace. She knew that she was going to die in this place. Still, she was upbeat and excited to see me and had made arrangements for us to have a special lunch together in the cafeteria.

The young girls in the cafeteria had made an effort to set up a more private table with a tablecloth and cloth napkins, as though we were in an expensive restaurant, and they waited on us, too. My aunt was so pleased. She knew that it was a game we were all playing…she knew it was the same cafeteria where she usually ate…but she was pleased that they had recognized that she had special company.

We luxuriated over a delicious salad, and a lovely lunch, and then a special dessert. We even had wine with our meal. Over coffee, served with a few wafers, I asked her about the story I had heard and could hardly believe. She giggled a conspiratorial laugh, and assured me that it was true. Every word.

She said that she had heard crude remarks, but had ignored them as uncouth, and, besides, who could imagine such a thing! She knew that animals, like cattle or cats did something and then gave birth in a bit of a bloody mess, but she assumed that humans didn't do any of that. Children were delivered rather neatly and, well, she had assumed that somehow the 'seed' was planted differently. Spread your legs? Good God, No! Never!

She said her wedding night was, indeed, a nightmare. She felt sorry that she embarrassed her poor dear husband, who had known she was naïve, but had never dreamed just how naïve she was. She said that she had secretly been nervous about pregnancy before they were married, because of some kissing, and she had noticed some changes in her husband as he had pressed against her…She told me with an accompanying gesture that once, on a double date with a girlfriend and her date, the girlfriend had instigated taking a peek in her own date's billfold, which he had left in the car when he and my soon to be uncle went to relieve themselves in the bushes after a dance. Both girls peeked and there was a little packet, which the other girl held up and giggled. My aunt asked, "But what is it?"

The boys were coming back and so the girl quickly returned it to the billfold and then made the rude gesture involving a circle made with finger and thumb of one hand with the third finger of the other hand moving in and out. Then the girl giggled and said, "You know!"

My aunt didn't know, she said. She giggled, too, however, because she knew that she was supposed to know something.

My aunt was making this gesture as she told me the story, and I happened to look up and I saw a stunned look on the face of the young girl who had been waiting on us. She didn't see me when I saw her reaction…I saw her surprise and then she ran off to the kitchen and in a moment she and another girl came out and moved closer to our table hoping, I believe, to hear what we were talking about. My aunt was unaware of our eavesdroppers, and she gaily went on telling me how she had asked her sister about the gesture, and that her sister suggested that she ask their mother…but she never did. It wasn't until her wedding night, when her young husband undressed, and she saw him naked, and he started to undress her, that she panicked and realized that there was a gap in her knowledge…and when she began to fill in what she knew about cats and cattle, she didn't like the idea much.

She said, "I had this beautiful pink nightie with lace and little flowers all over it, and he wanted me to take it off, so it wouldn't get ruined!

I thought, 'how could it get ruined?' and that is when I realized what I hadn't put together, and I ran into the bathroom, locked the door and started to cry. Then I didn't want to come out because I thought, 'I am such a ninny! Why didn't I know this!' and then I cried harder, and my face was puffy and red and my nightie was getting wet from tears! Oh, what a night! And then Richard asked me if he could call my mother! I said, 'yes', of course. But imagine, I was 24 and my new husband had to call my mother so she could calm me down about having sex on my wedding night!"

We both giggled like fools with each other, and the young girls were giggling, too, just out of sight of my aunt!

My aunt hadn't grown up in a tower...

And, as far as I know, my aunt was never obviously 'betrayed'...

In the two versions of The Girl With No Hands, the girl is betrayed first by a male family member and then, in a different way, by her husband who believes, too quickly, the lies that are told about her.

In Rapunzel, first her father betrays her by giving her up to the witch and then the young man, the 'prince', betrays her by failing to comprehend her narrowed world view, and, indeed, only thinking of himself. How could Rapunzel, sequestered in a lonely tower, know and understand the consequences of sexual intercourse?

In some versions, Rapunzel reveals that she has a secret visitor by innocently commenting on the difference between how slowly the witch climbs her hair and how quickly her visitor climbs her hair. If she were truly devious, she would not have made that comment to the witch! If she had understood that the witch was keeping her away from others for a reason…that the witch thought that she was protecting her, perhaps…safeguarding her innocence? If she truly understood the consequences of allowing the young man into her life, she would not have so casually mentioned him! What would she have imagined to be the result of such a revelation? What might have been her 'back-up' plan? Young man versus Witch…arm-wrestling? Pistols at twenty paces?

And what was the witch's plan anyway? Do we know? Did she think that things would stay this way forever? Maybe just for one hundred years, as in Sleeping Beauty…or maybe she did not fully comprehend that, although things stay the same at first, because boys and girls are pretty much alike as children, then, suddenly, things change no matter what an authority figure, witch or religion or government, determines to do. Menses begin, breasts develop…and females emerge as the powerful, life-creating forces that everyone, secretly, no matter how well concealed it might be under the prevailing cultural burka, knows to be true…and then…

Betrayal. Because of fear? Because of self-interest? Because of a need to feel powerful?

I liked to play on a large open corner of the school playground when I was in elementary school. I was a year younger than the other students in my grade, and I was slender and a 'late-bloomer'. One day I was pawing the ground and throwing back my head, whinnying like a horse, as I galloped around in that corner of the play yard. It was grassy there and made a perfect meadow, or, perhaps I was seeing it as the wide prairie out west and that I was a wild pony…at any rate, I didn't notice a cadre of children edging into 'my' prairie.

I wasn't self-conscious about pretending to be a horse. I actually thought that I was pretty good at being a horse and was a little proud of it. If I had fully noticed the other children, I would have hoped that they would join me and then we would be a herd of wild horses thundering across the plains…

As it turned out, that wasn't their intent. They were being herded close to me by a maverick and a mean-spirited maverick at that. Her name was Deena, and she was fairly new to the area. She had moved into town during the summer, while I was gone to camp, and she had interwoven herself into a whole web of friendships with the children who lived close to each other in a different part of the town where I lived. I had not paid much attention to her because she was boy crazy and clothes crazy and style crazy, and I wasn't any of those things. I still wanted to be a horse.

I was galloping close to them when Deena called to me, and, still in my horse persona, I stopped, turned my head a bit to see them better and then, foolishly, trotted over to them.

Deena began by asking me what I was doing. I told her that I was a horse. Deena began to laugh at me, and she was joined by a few of the other children. I shook my pretend mane and turned to gallop off, but I fell instead. The children had crowded up around me and someone tripped me. I put out my arms to catch myself, and, apparently, my hand hit Deena's breast as I went down.

Deena began to screech, "Did you see where she hit me? Did you all see it? Nobody can hit me there and get away with it! Hold her!"

And, like frightened sheep, several of the children, children whom I had know all my life, held me while Deena proceeded to 'knuckle rub' my barely budding breasts. The school bell rang and all the children broke and ran to line up to go inside. Deena also got to her feet and said, "Never disobey me again! And never touch me again!" and then she, too, ran to get into line.

Lying in the grass, none of the teachers saw me as they rounded up everyone else and marched then into school to start their classes again.

I lay there for a few minutes watching the clouds drift overhead, until I was certain that everyone was inside, and then I sat up. My blouse was badly wrinkled and stained. It looked like dirt or mud. Most of it was right where my swollen nipples were aching under the material.

I was shaking. My legs felt weak, and I struggled to my feet and headed drunkenly toward the school building. I was trying to make some sense out of what had happened, but I couldn't. By the time I reached the school doors, I had begun to formulate a plan. I would sneak in to the girl's bathroom while everyone was in class and wash my face and hands, then I would go down to the nurse's office and tell the nurse that I had fallen down and that I felt sick and that I wanted to go home.

My father came to get me as the nurse said that she thought I might have hit my head on the pavement of the playground closest to the school. That was her invention, because I just said that I had been running and that I fell, but I couldn't remember where on the playground I had been...

I told my father part of the truth. I told him that Deena and some other children had pushed me down, and I had gotten dirty and that I just wanted to go home. My father asked me if I felt dizzy, and I said, "No" and I added that I hadn't hit my head, that I just let the nurse think that so I could go home. My father said that he would take me home. He suggested that I might take a bath and relax and maybe I would feel better. He said that my mother would be home soon and that he needed to get back to the store.

That sounded fine to me. I went up the back stairs and into our apartment. I was sitting in the bathtub when my mother got home. I was feeling better. I had washed my chest carefully because I was so very sore. By that time I had realized that the stain on my blouse that I had thought was mud actually had been blood, and that the blood had come from my nipples.

My mother came into the bathroom, and I turned a little away from her so she couldn't see my chest. She picked up my blouse and said, "I had better try to get these stains out before they set."

She began to scrub at my blouse in the sink next to me. Suddenly she stopped and said, "This isn't dirt!" She knelt down next to the bathtub and took hold of my shoulder and turned my chest toward her. I turned my head away, awash with shame.

She gasped. "How did this happen!" I began to cry and finally I blubbered out the story.

By that evening my chest was black and blue. My parents took me to see Dr. Lewis…another humiliating moment for me, although he was as gentle a man as could be. He had a long conversation with my parents, but I have no idea what was said. I know that I had to return to school and that Deena seemed smug. I don't remember pretending to be a horse again.

******

My husband and I moved from a city to a town, to a city to a village to a farm to a town to a city and, then, off to yet another small town. This town was in a very isolated area in the western plains states. Our children were fascinated with the new freedoms that came with returning to living in a smaller community. They had loved the farm and the small town we had left in the Midwest. This new small town felt familiar, more familiar to them than the city had ever felt. Immediately they unpacked their bikes and set out to explore their new territory. First they went around the block, noting all the houses and street names and curious looks…and then they set out to look for other children in the next block. I was busy with the younger children who were still restricted to the driveway with their tricycles.

It wasn't long before the older ones were back. Oh, they had seen a few children in the next block, but, there was no sidewalk and so they had ridden their bicycles over the weedy grass that was next to the road and somehow, one by one, they had blown their tires! They hadn't seen any nails, but they certainly had flat tires.

I was annoyed because tire tubes are expensive and, besides, we had unpacking to do and having the biggest children repairing their bicycles all day meant that things were going to go even more slowly than I had imagined.

"Put your bikes in the garage and help me unpack for a while. Are you sure your tires are flat, not just low on air? Did you ride through a construction area? How could all of your tires be flat at once?" I queried.

They came inside and grumpily began to help unpack, but it wasn't long before some of the children they had spotted in the next block came wheeling past our house.

"There are children out there!" one of my boys whispered to the others.

Everyone ran to the windows. The local children quickly took off on their bikes and rode on down the road a little way.

"Don't worry," I consoled. "They will come back. Maybe you should go outside and move some of the boxes around in the garage. I really am looking for a box of pots and pans that doesn't seem to be here in the kitchen."

All of the children rushed toward the back door and managed to squeeze through. The younger ones squatted in the yard and just stared at the children who were watching us from down the block. The older children began to dutifully search through the unopened boxes in the garage, while stealing glances down the street.

One of my girls ran in to give me a progress report…No Pots and Pan box yet, and The Watchers had moved back closer to us.

"Give them time," I suggested. "Then one of you can wave to them and maybe they will see that you are friendly and come on in the driveway." I kept on unpacking.

Just as I had predicted, the watcher children began to drift closer and finally one boy came all the way to the entrance to our driveway.

"We saw your bikes," he said.

My children stopped their rummaging among the boxes and looked at him. One of my boys said, "Yeah. We got flat tires, now."

The watcher boy said, "Where you from?"

My boys told him where we had been living just before this move.

The watcher boy was quiet. He was thinking. Then he said, "Maybe they don't got thorns there where you lived. You got to have thorn-proof tires here."

My children looked at each other in consternation. Thorn-proof tires? Who ever heard of that? For that matter, who ever heard of thorns that could puncture a tire?

We quickly learned that we shouldn't go bare-foot there either. We didn't have thorn proof feet. Thorns.

One of my sons whose tires were pierced on that day by those thorns, has found that learning about the thorns of each place in the world is an important skill. Once, he and his wife moved into a very isolated area in south central Pennsylvania. He was working for an agency that had earned a somewhat negative reputation with the local people, and he was trying to restore some good will. He and his wife decided that they would have to go out of their way to try to meet their new neighbors, since their neighbors were avoiding them. They bravely baked cookies and packaged them up and set out to confront the nearest homes with friendly offerings. No one was home at the first house. No one was home at the second house. My son's wife was getting a little annoyed. At the third house, there was the sound of growling and vicious barking coming from a rickety kennel and then, as they knocked at the door, a voice called out, "I've got a gun!!"

And my daughter-in-law answered, "Well, we've got cookies!"

Thorn-proofing.

Okay...Got to dive underwater. After years of wandering hopelessly, Rapunzel's lover stumbles blindly into the same remote desert where Rapunzel has been eking out a living, just barely surviving. And Rapunzel has borne children—twins. The witch, upon discovering that Rapunzel had been meeting her lover secretly, had driven the frightened and pregnant teenager away from the tower, the only home she had known.

Rapunzel would have had no idea what had happened to her lover. And to find herself pregnant? Would she have known she was pregnant? She had been kept away from the world! Her lover was the one who knew the possible consequences of their love, but he apparently didn't think beyond his own immediate desires. What must she have thought and felt?

Even though the old woman was a 'witch', Rapunzel wouldn't have known her that way, unless her lover had told her thus. But where was he, anyway. She had no way of knowing if he was looking for her, or not. She would only have known that the witch found her unacceptable and vile now that she had been 'defiled'.

Tough stuff for this sheltered teenager.

A man six years my senior began to flirt with me when I was a teenager, and I was flattered. Everyone warned me that he was trouble, but I was so used to being ridiculed and teased by these same people, that I rather enjoyed having them wonder just what this 'older man' saw in me. Besides, he denied that he had done anything bad. Instead, he said that people blamed him because his older sister had had some problems…but now she was fine, too. But people just wouldn't leave the family alone…

I believed him. Besides he had had an eye injury as a child and was blind in one eye. Why did people pick on him so? He said that he had wanted to go into the service so that he could afford to go to college, but he had been turned down because of his blind eye…

I believed him. I believed him. My parents forbade me to see him. I met him in secret. I overlooked things that he did. I made excuses for him. I thought that people were unfair to him. I defended him up until the night I met him wearing my new red gloves. They were beautiful leather gloves with rabbit fur lining and the prettiest red color I had ever seen. They were a gift to me from someone I think now was a true friend…but I didn't know about true friends then.

It was a snowy night. I remember that. I had met this man, and I was with him in his car. He suggested that we go for a drive out to see the snow in the woods. I couldn't have been happier at the thought of driving out to see the soft, white snow coating the dark branches of the barren trees. Gentle snow coming down. The light wind swirling it over the road. The quiet woods. He parked the car, and I moved to get out. I wanted to breathe in the crisp air and scuff through the light snow with my boots, and I wanted to feel my fingers warm in my red gloves.

He had no intention of letting me out of the car. As I tried to pull away and open the door, he slammed my head against the passenger side window and then trapped my head between the door armrest and the seat. A lot of kicking and screaming and thrashing, but he was twice my size, maybe more, and he had me securely trapped. He let me out of the car when I started to choke on my vomit.

That must be when I lost the glove.

We rode back to town in silence. I had stopped vomiting, and I was no longer crying. A month or so later I saw him again, and I said that I thought I might be pregnant. I, at least, knew what that was. I had read about the symptoms in my high school health class. I expected that he would suggest that we get married. I was young, but a few other girls in my class had married because they were pregnant. It was embarrassing, but...

He told me that I was frigid, and he had no intention of marrying a girl who was frigid, and, anyway, he had a new girlfriend.

From that point on, my life was chaos. My parent's lawyer sued that 'older man' for damages...for my parents, because I was now 'damaged'. The lawyer then arranged for me to be incarcerated in a home for unwed mothers. I was driven out of the tower, a frightened pregnant teenager.

Swimming. I want to keep my head above the water now. I saw more than one psychiatrist throughout this time of my late teenage and early young adulthood years. One of them suggested that, perhaps, the safest I had ever felt in my life was when I was swimming in the womb of my mother. I think that there is something to that idea.

The home for unwed mothers was anything but a 'home'. It was a red brick hospital where, on the lower levels, wealthy women from nearby communities could be well-attended by their doctors when it was time for them to deliver their babies. They needn't go to the large general hospitals in the city. They could go to the "Maternity Hospital'. How very nice for them. I don't know if they realized that on the top floor there were dormitory type rooms for those of us who had been rejected and abandoned.

We did much of the work of the hospital. Each girl was given a job in one of three places: the laundry, the nursery, or the kitchen. I was assigned the kitchen. I asked for the nursery, because, I said, I thought that I was going to keep my baby, and I needed to learn more about the care of babies. I didn't understand that one of the unstated purposes of this institution was to supply babies to adoption agencies, one in particular, and that my announcement of my intent to consider keeping my child merely confirmed their suspicions that I should be kept away from the babies.

How, in an atmosphere of rejection and shame, did I even consider keeping my child? It wasn't a simple desire. I agonized over that decision. I did not, at that time, realize that the legal suit would only benefit my parents. I didn't know that persons under a certain age have few, if any, legal rights. I thought that I would have a certain sum of money from the lawsuit to help with caring for my child. I thought that my parents would continue their support of me, at least until I finished college. They had always told me that I was expected to go to college and that they expected to pay for that. I was a 4 point student on a 4 point scale, so I thought I might have some scholarship money to help with my education, too.

As far as the rejection I endured, being called frigid and unmarriageable; well, perhaps it was true. This child would be my only child in that case. And it was my child, emphasis on 'my', because that 'older man' was out of the picture so quickly, that I hardly associated the growing child with the terrible night of the red gloves and the ugly, attacking wolf.

Gradually I became convinced that I could keep my child and survive. Perhaps I would have to go to night school, or delay school a few years, but I knew of other women who went back to school when their children were a little older. I was already taking correspondence courses from the University, and I had gotten A's! I could do this!

The second floor of the 'Home' was the delivery floor, nursery floor and recovery room floor. There were two wings—well separated. One wing was for the well-heeled married women and the other wing was for the rest of us. I was a frequent visitor to both wings because my kitchen job included taking trays of meals up to the ladies. This privilege meant that I had access to a rather nice balcony, also. I didn't discover this spot right away because, even though I delivered meals on that floor on a regular basis, nevertheless, I wasn't supposed to be wandering around there between meals because the nursery for all the babies was on that floor, too.

Girls who had already signed away their babies were allowed to work in the nursery, and, therefore could be on that floor, but most of those girls stayed hidden and didn't explore around, because they were afraid that someone, a visitor of the married women, perhaps, might recognize them—and figure out that "so and so's daughter isn't really visiting relatives on the west coast". I didn't care about that. I intended to go home with a baby anyway, so if someone in my hometown saw me, big deal. They would know soon enough if they didn't know already.

At any rate, I had discovered the balcony. No one seemed to go there, although I thought it was quite nice. It offered a wonderful view of the trees and yards of the surrounding neighborhoods. It was quiet and peaceful there. Sometimes I took a book with me and sat in the sun. I usually had to settle myself in a corner with my back against the sun-warmed bricks of the building in order to stay out of sight from anyone, a nurse or administrator, perhaps, who might walk past the glass French doors that led out to the balcony.

I kept the balcony as my secret place. When the other girls were sitting in the lounge, or in the 'pen' (the fenced in area in the back of the building), smoking and talking or reading magazines, I would creep up to the balcony.

As if the second story of the balcony of an old-style hospital weren't high enough for a somewhat off-balance pregnant teenager, I used that balcony as a means to climb up on the roof. I was tempting fate. I was so very unhappy, and I felt so terribly rejected. Everything, from the shapeless white uniform we were forced to wear, to the way we were made to stand in line for our prenatal vitamins, worked to impress upon all of us that we were worthless, 'rejects'. If we had been worthy, someone would have wanted us, married us, helped us through our pregnancies…like the husbands we saw coming in to visit their wives on the second floor. Those women had some value. They deserved to have their Babies brought to them for them to hold and cuddle. Our babies needed to be given to someone like those women. We were obviously not capable of loving or caring for our babies otherwise.

After a few days which had led me to feel especially unwanted, and unattractive and incompetent, I crept to the balcony and from there up to the roof above the married women's wing. I remember sitting on the slate tiles and looking out from this higher vantage point and wondering if I should just let go and fall. I remember that it was autumn by that time, and I could see miles and miles of orange and red and yellow leaves mixed with the dark greens of the pines. In the distance I could see the glittering buildings of the city. I felt as though I were on the prow of a boat, and the many colored leaves were brightly colored fishes...I wished myself dead, but I couldn't wish my child dead, and so I carefully returned to the balcony.

My child was born, and I managed to take care of her from 1 AM until dawn everyday for the last week I was in the hospital. During the day I slept and waited, because the day nurses refused to let me care for her. But the night nurse held a different philosophy...When I was alone with my child, I even tried to nurse her.

At the end of the week, my child was whisked off to a foster home and from there to an adoptive home. It turned out that I had had no choice after all. I had no say in the decision about adoption. I was lied to by my parents, the lawyer and the social workers. My child was taken, and I was thrown out, back into the society that judged me as damaged goods and nothing more.

After this experience, I wandered hopelessly and despairingly. I was an outsider everywhere. I did not return to my home and parents. I felt I could not.

I found that I was surrounded by people who were enjoying being young. I did not feel young. Everywhere I looked, I saw people who had families and each other. I felt removed from the world I had lived in all my life, and I had no idea if there was a place for me anywhere. I felt as though I were looking out through a window at life, and that I was forever locked away from it.

I spent the next twenty years waiting.

How long did Rapunzel wait? Were her children still young? I don't know. Like Rapunzel, I did go on living. I married. I had a family. I cooked and cleaned. I even finished college.

And, as I have mentioned, as I approached my fortieth year, I began to swim. It was as though something began to thaw. I think, perhaps, that the 'swarthy man' had given his sleepy medicine to me and then, he gave a dose of 'wakeup' medicine to me. I began to remember things that I had loved. I remembered how I had loved to learn about insects. I remembered that I had enjoyed Latin. Things that had been lost in dim corners of my life began to push their way to the surface.

One summer, when several of my children were in their middle growing up years, my parents came to visit. Earlier in my marriage I had avoided my parents. Once they drove almost two thousand miles to see us for what was supposed to be a week-long visit and, instead, they left on the second day because they could not tolerate my politics. One of my boys had turned down the volume when the National Anthem was sung before a baseball game. It was during the Vietnam War, and both my husband and I were anti-war and, to us, playing a national anthem before a ball game seemed a little reminiscent of Hitler. At any rate, our son was merely doing what he had seen his father do, but my mother was outraged at his unpatriotic behavior. I asked her to be tolerant of our views and ways of doing things, but she had gotten stuck, and so they packed up their things and left. My son was bereft because he felt that he was at fault. He knew that I longed to be accepted by my parents. We had cleaned house and made up a room for them a week before they were to arrive, and I had baked and cooked and waited for their arrival…

And so it was that things had not been healed between us yet when they called to say that they were traveling west and thought they might stop by to spend a few days. I was anxious, but once again I hoped that it would be a good visit. I hoped that my children could have some kind of relationship with my family. I wanted them to know what it was to have grandparents, and my husband's parents were gone…

My parents arrived and things were somewhat tense, but the children were delighted and warm and their presence seemed to help things go smoothly. It was July, and my older children were preparing their 4-H projects for the local fair. Several of them had insect collections, just like I had had so many years before. I told my father that we needed to make display boxes for the children and that I had gone to the lumber yard and gotten the wood for them, but hadn't had time to help the children to put them together. I wondered if he could help them, and he was delighted. He busied himself with sawing and sanding and constructing those boxes according to the dimensions required, and then he said that he needed to go into town to get the glass for the tops and the stain for the constructed boxes. He took the measurements-and the children-and they headed into town to go to the lumber yard.

They came back and, one-by-one, finished the boxes. The children came in to report that Grandpa had shown them how to stain their own boxes and was just finishing the last box. Did I want to come see them?

"Of course," I said. Out I went to see the workshop area that my father had set up in our yard. The finished boxes were lined up, and he had only one box that still needed to be stained. I admired the finished boxes and complimented each child on their staining prowess. But there was the one unstained box. Everyone looked at me expectantly.

"But you've made an extra box!" I commented as I looked over the boxes and each child that had claimed them.

"I thought that you might like one, too," my father said.

"But you have to stain it yourself, Mama!" giggled the children.

I looked at my father, and he looked down at the box, embarrassed at my emotion. Then I excused myself to run back into the house and put on 'old clothes' before staining the last box.

My box.

My mother was not particularly well at the time of this visit, and, what seemed to be bothering her most was her eyesight. Her good eye was failing. She had many 'floaters' and things were blurry much of the time. She had always loved to read and to do puzzles, crosswords and jigsaw and such, and now even those small pleasures were becoming difficult.

I tried to monitor my reactions as she talked about her frustrations concerning her eyesight. She seemed oblivious to my feelings of guilt. In front of me, if she had mentioned the incident of the thorn at all, she had always insisted that it had been an accident and that I had nothing to do with her loss.

But deep in my memory, there was something I had tried to bury. I thought that I remembered that when those adults were crowded around her, and the Doctor was explaining that she was probably experiencing a 'sympathetic reaction', and that her eyesight in her uninjured eye would probably come back... I thought that she had cried out, "Why did she do this to me?" Did I imagine that? Whether I imagined it or not, I do remember that, at some point in time that evening, my father took me to my room and told me to stay there, and he said that my mother was delirious and had been given many pain killers and that she was hysterical. I don't remember his exact words, of course, but he told me something like that.

I do remember hearing her as she moaned and sobbed all that night, and I heard people coming in and out of the house to care for her. I sat in my room, listening. I sat there and took on all that guilt and shame and remorse.

I told my mother that I had always felt responsible that she had lost her eyesight in her right eye, and that I felt terrible that she was now having so much trouble with her good eye. She was shocked. I really think she hadn't known this. She said, again and again, that, of course, it had been an accident, and that I had managed to get her home…and we left it at that.

The odd thing is that her regular eye doctor, an older man who had taken care of her for years, retired. My mother was upset and reluctant to meet the new, young ophthalmologist. Finally she made an appointment to see him because her eyesight had grown so bad that she was nearly blind. She thought that perhaps he could strengthen her glasses again. She was desperate.

She went to see him, and he examined her old records. He checked her failing eye. He pondered it all. Then he said, "Tell me about your right eye. How did you lose your eyesight in that eye," and she told him the story.

He said, "Let me have a look at it". Then, after checking her injured eye, he said, "You know, we now have something called laser surgery, and I think this eye could be repaired. It wouldn't be perfect, but it could be a way of keeping you from total blindness."

And it was. My mother called me to tell me that she was going to have a new surgery and that it would repair some of that old injury.

For me it repaired all of the old injury. I felt, as they say, 'a weight lift from my heart'. I hadn't even realized how heavy that weight had been all those years. Healing tears, Rapunzel. I had never believed the end of the story where Rapunzel, reunited with her long-lost lover, weeps, and her tears fall into his thorn-pierced, blinded eyes and heals them.

******

Most of my pregnancies were uneventful, except for silly things such as the time our dog jumped on me, and I fell backwards into the snow and couldn't get up again. Like a turtle on its back, I was! My husband and the children just stood around me laughing as I thrashed and wriggled, and our dear old dog licked my face and sniffed at my mittened hands.

One pregnancy was a bit more challenging, however, because, when I tried to push a car out of a snow bank, I ruptured one layer of the amniotic 'bag of waters' and ended up on bed rest for almost five months. My daughter was born, healthy and feisty and beautiful, unaware that I had been worried about her for more than half the time she was developing inside me. And I set out to try to nurse her. I had never had much success with nursing, and I was determined to succeed this time.

I was propped up in bed, daughter cupped up to my breast, when my husband stormed in and began to rant and rave about something. I don't remember what had upset him …all I remember is that I grew so annoyed with him that I looked up and said, "Now you did it! Now I have to have another baby!"

We both stopped and listened to the echo of my words…Another baby? We already had eight children counting his daughter from a first marriage and not counting my first child…what was this 'have to have another baby' business? I was holding a newborn!

I gave it some deep thought and up bubbled an idea. Perhaps I had more children than anyone I knew because some part of me was trying to repair an old injury to my psyche--something that had occurred during that first pregnancy. A friend suggested a therapist, an older woman, and she and I began to talk. It was intense. I decided that I had an imaginary idea in my head about what a 'perfect pregnancy' should be…no stress, no bickering, no fatigue, no adoption, no rejection, etc., etc.   Just as I was beginning to feel that I could deal with my earlier loss, and have a more relaxed view of my choices and simply enjoy my family… my husband brought in a letter from the mailbox. It was from a social worker who had found a letter I had written to her agency six years before, when my first child would have been thirteen. My letter had been an update with my address and phone number in case my daughter ever visited the agency and asked about me.

My daughter had done just that, and the social worker wanted to know if I wanted to be reunited with her.

Several months later, after the social worker had reunited the two of us at the agency, miles away from where I lived, my daughter of nineteen asked if she might fly out to meet her brothers and sisters, and their father, her step-father. We all journeyed to the airport to meet her plane.

My other children were excited and eager to meet her. They had all tried to dress up so they could look their best...except one son. He was fourteen. He insisted on wearing a bandana around his forehead, jeans that were ripped up one side and tied together with three or four bandanas and a button-less flannel shirt. He had a well-practiced sullen look on this face. My husband had at first started to insist that his son change into something more appropriate, but I stopped him.

"Let him wear what he wants," I said. "It is his sister. This is the way he wants to meet her."

We waited as the plane landed and the passengers emerged from the tunnel. It seemed as though hundreds of passengers walked past us. Then there was a pause when no one came out. For one horrible moment I thought that she had changed her mind, and then she stepped out and began to make her way toward us. Her brothers and sisters began to push forward to hug her and tell her their names…all except my fourteen year old son. He held back.

My oldest daughter began to smile as she started to try to sort out just which name went with which person. Then she confronted my son. "You must be Tim. And I guess I don't have to hide this anymore," and out from behind her ear she flipped out the longest 'rattail' that I had ever seen.

Tim's eyes widened in appreciation, and he said, "Whoa!" Then all of us walked back to the car, the younger ones skipping beside her, the older ones asking questions, and Tim just grinning with pleasure.

Sometime after I was reunited with my daughter, I found that I was pregnant again. I didn't expect 'a perfect pregnancy' anymore. I didn't need one. Things were healing in my soul. This child, another daughter, was born while my parents were visiting, and they, both, even my father, were able to hold this tiny newborn soon after she arrived.

There were other challenges, though. We moved to a city eight hours away from our small town home. We were only to be there a few years, so we had rented a place. Not easy for such a large family. And we moved when the new baby was only a few weeks old. Once again the nursing I had so wished to do was failing. My husband's job kept him away most of the day, and I was alone with the other children in a strange city with a tiny baby that, suddenly, didn't seem to be doing very well. I had so hoped to nurse the way other women seemed to be able to nurse this time. I was over forty. I wouldn't have another chance. I decided to see if there would be anyone who could help me before I gave up again.

I called the La Leche League number from the paper and something in my voice must have touched the woman to whom I spoke. She was a lactation consultant. She urged me to find a pediatrician. I explained that I was new, that I had no transportation, and that I was worried about my baby. She came over to my house, and without alarming me, arranged for me to try to use a 'supplementer'…a device which held formula but was taped to my breasts so my baby could nurse and get fed. I was producing very little milk, and she couldn't see why, but my child needed to be nourished, so, with a pediatrician's permission, we could try this method of feeding while we figured out why I wasn't able to nurse. She went with me to see the pediatrician.

After all those births, and all those attempts at nursing, I finally succeeded. For several months I needed to use that device…because the milk I finally was producing was not from the badly damaged milk glands beneath my nipples. There are other milk glands in the breast, and even in the upper arms, and eventually those glands began to produce milk, and my baby continued to nurse and thrive. Another mystery solved. Another healing for me.

My mother was diagnosed with Parkinson's Disease, then she fell and was hospitalized and finally my father was forced to place her in a nursing home where he could visit her every day. I began to fly back to visit them on a more regular basis. My father was in his eighties and my brother lived close by to help him most of the year, but he was also glad when I could come and stay with my father and spend time with my mother so that he and his family could go on trips or simply take a break. It was during this time that my mother and I renewed our earlier attachments.

My father was afraid to take her out of the nursing home. He was afraid of driving anywhere with her, even over to their house, and my brother and his family were usually too busy to take her out except when she had medical appointments. But I had the time, and I was highly motivated. I packed her into the car with her wheelchair in the trunk and tucked my father in next to her, and I took them to the state park. We looked for deer. We got out and sat at a picnic table. I showed her how to blow on a water reed to make a shrill whistle. I had her blowing dandelion tops when she could barely blow out to make a whispered word.

I took her shopping. I took her to the library. I took her to the pet shop to see the baby guinea pigs. I took her out to a place I remembered where there were wild raspberries. My father rode along on most of these ventures, but not all of them. Sometimes he took a nap while my mother and I went out. She couldn't talk, except for a few very soft, almost completely unintelligible words, but we laughed together and enjoyed the crisp air in autumn, and the warm air in the spring.

During this time I noticed that my insect boxes from the collections I had made as a child were still hanging on the wall. I commented that I was surprised that they were in such good shape. "Oh," my father said, "Your mother put moth balls in them every six months clear up until she couldn't do that anymore, and then I started to do it for her. She was determined to protect them for you."

When my mother died, my father gave me a letter that she had written years before. She had put it in her things and told him that if she died first that she wanted him to give it to me. It was a revelation to me. It was all about how she had been terrified of 'creepy things' such as insects and worms and frogs. She had only loved flowers. When I was little she realized that I had a fascination with these other things, and she didn't want me to know how she felt, so she had determined to keep it a secret from me! She wrote, "I tried so hard not to let it show how frightened I was of the frog you would try to hand me, or the caterpillar you would ask me to hold for you! Did you know?"

No, I told my father. I didn't know. I had always thought that I got my love of nature from her, because she always encouraged me to explore the world around me! My father said, "It was her great secret! I know she is smiling!"

I began to drive my father back and forth to Florida where he and my mother had had a little trailer that they had enjoyed during the winter for the years before she became so ill. He had wanted to sell the trailer when my mother died, but my brother and I convinced him to keep it as we thought that he might want to return to Florida sometime. He had always enjoyed being able to get outside and ride his bike around the trailer court and visit with his neighbors when he was down there, and that seemed like that might be a good thing for him to do again.

At first my brother drove down with him in the fall, and I would drive him back in the spring, but in between he would stay by himself. He had a group of friends and enjoyed the mild weather and all seemed to be going well. As my children grew older, I found that I could spend a little more time in Florida with my father. Finally, all of my children except my youngest daughter were off to various schools, and I found that she and I could go and spend a whole month or so with him in Florida and then we would drive back north again at a leisurely pace.

One time we decided that we would try to stop and visit my cousin, the cousin with whom I had had 'fun' hiding from her father out in the woods. I hadn't heard from her for many years except once when I had taken my father to her mother's funeral. I remember that I selfishly had searched among the mourners to see her, now an older adult, weeping for her mother along with her sisters.

I learned that she had moved her parents to live close to where she had lived for so many years in the western part of South Carolina. But the funeral wasn't the moment for renewing friendships. There was an old family struggle tugging at all of them as insidiously as an undertow current, just beneath the surface of the funeral. All three sisters were present but one sister would not even look at her father. Her anger and pain were evident to everyone who knew them. I hugged each one and gave my condolences, and vowed to myself that I would find a way to reconnect with Juanita.

When the opportunity came, I was excited. Juanita had sounded pleased when we spoke over the phone and made our plans. My youngest daughter was with my father and me on that trip, and I was anxious for her to meet Juanita, too.

Juanita had insisted that we meet her at the sandwich shop that she owned and ran and suggested that we could eat our supper there and then follow her home where we could spend the night. My father thought that we should get a motel room, but Juanita was adamant. If we went to a motel, we wouldn't have enough time to visit.

We found the sandwich shop, and I felt as though I were an overexcited puppy, I was so eager to see her. We ate our sandwiches, and she chatted with us in between customers. There was one man who sat in a booth by himself for most of the time we were there, until Juanita went over to him, and spoke to him. He shook his head, and she shrugged, but went back to the kitchen. I was curious, so I followed her back and said, "So who is the man?"

She laughed, and said, "He is my guardian angel. I've been stabbed and robbed three times here in this shop, just as it is getting close to closing time. I've known him for years, and he comes over to sit in the shop until I close on the nights when I don't have anyone else here to help. He just does it because he figures as long as it looks like I'm not here alone it will be OK. I put up this plexiglass to protect myself, and I usually have other workers here at night, but like tonight, I didn't have anyone scheduled, so he asked me about it when he came for his dinner and then he just stayed. I told him that you folks were staying, but he figured that you don't look very scary, I guess!"

Stabbed and robbed three times. I said, "Juanita, I never heard about this!"

"Cause I didn't tell anyone. This is the way I support myself. I'm not ready to retire yet."

215

We waited until Juanita was closing, and then as we went to our car, I nodded good-bye to Juanita's guardian angel, who nodded back, picked up his newspaper and waited until Juanita was safely in her car before he headed off to his home.

I asked Juanita if he was more than a guardian angel, but she denied it. She said that she paid him with a free sandwich and since he ate there every night, being a watch dog for her now and then for a free sandwich was a good deal.

Stabbed three times.

Juanita's house was way back on a winding road among the trees. There was a little fishing pond just down from her back door. We no sooner drove in than my young daughter galloped down to the pond, and Juanita called out to her, "You want a fishin' pole? There's crappies a'plenty in that pond!"

My daughter nodded, and Juanita set her up with a pole, some bait and a bucket of water for the fish she assured my daughter that she would catch.

"I'll clean them for your breakfast," Juanita said. My daughter was enthralled. It was a magical place, where you could just put in your line, wait a minute and then you could pull out a fish. And that is just what happened.

In the meantime Juanita set out to show us where to put our overnight things. She showed my father to a pleasant little guest bedroom, and then she showed me into a little room which was full of odds and ends including a place for a sewing machine and a table covered with an assortment of acorns and rocks and various items from nature. She laughed and confided, "I still like stuff like this."

I assured her that I did, too. Then she pulled back a curtain to reveal a hole cut into the wall about five feet up from the floor. There was a bed made up in that hole, and she moved a ladder over to it. "I call it my squirrel nest, and I sleep there in the winter. Do you think your daughter would like to sleep there?"

I knew my daughter would be delighted to sleep in a squirrel nest in a room full of squirrel things.

Finally Juanita showed me to the bedroom where I was to sleep. "Juanita," I said. This house has lots of bedrooms!"

"It's big enough," she agreed. "Too big now that the children are gone."

Juanita's husband had left quite a while before, and she had raised her two children by herself, supporting them with the money from the sandwich shop.

When I had settled Kate in the squirrel nest, and my father had retired for the night, Juanita and I had a chance to reminisce and catch up on our lives. As we sat in front of her fireplace with a tiny fire before us, it felt familiar. I looked around the room lazily and realized that every corner still had autumn leaves in it. The woodpile for the fire was shedding onto the stone floor. There were crickets chirping inside. I could hear the frogs in the nearby pond, and Kate's breakfast fish were splashing in the bucket in the near-by kitchen.

I was exhausted from the trip, and my head was buzzing with memories and thoughts and feelings. As we said, "Good night" at last, and I headed for my room, I realized that I wasn't certain where Juanita's room was. "Juanita," I said, "where are you sleeping?"

She laughed, "I thought I was gonna get away with it! Come on. I'll show you where I sleep."

I followed her to a sliding door that led out onto a narrow balcony. An old mattress was leaning against the wall. Juanita pointed to the mattress. "I sleep on that out here, with a few blankets, because I love to hear all the night critters as I fall asleep."

******

Reunions. Healing Tears. Everything seems to happen for a reason. As I grew older my own vision began to dim. I thought that my glasses were smudged, and I cleaned them and examined them again and again. I hated to think that I needed new glasses, because the ones I had were only a year old. My daughter grew impatient with me and made an appointment for me with her optometrist. "I'll pay for any new glasses, if you need them!" she said. And off we went to see her optometrist.

He was concerned. "Yes," he confirmed, "you need a new prescription. But," he added, "there is something else going on in your eye. Do you have high blood pressure? Perhaps you are having fluctuations of blood pressure, and that is damaging your vision."

I was glad to have the new glasses. They did help. But now I was worried about my blood pressure! I went to see my regular doctor who became thoughtful. "You've never had what I would consider a high pressure reading…and why would only one eye be affected if it is truly a blood pressure problem?" And so I went to see yet another eye specialist.

This man was a very young man with an easy grin. He examined me and used a very special, top-of-the-line, computer-image generating tool of some sort and was delighted to announce that he could clearly see the source of the problem. I had an epiretinal membrane covering the retina of my right eye. I had a slight one on my left eye, too, but the one on my right eye was, clearly, the vision dimming culprit.

I was horrified. "Epiretinal membrane. Covering my retina!" I whispered in shock.

He continued, as he gazed at the computer image on the screen, "Oh, this is good news! It is completely repairable now. The retinologists have a completely new method of correcting this type of thing. They make three little holes in your eye, remove the fluid, while putting different fluid in, then they use a special tiny tool to scrap the membrane off the retina…"

At this point he looked up at me, and his smile turned to surprise as he saw the look on my face. "Oh, maybe I shouldn't have said so much!" he apologized.

"Well," I gasped, "at the part where you said 'they make three little holes in your eye', I think I blacked out!" Then I managed a tentative laugh to reassure him that I was recovering.

"Really," he continued, "this is good news. It can be fixed. It is a surgery that has been tested, and it works. I will give you the name of a surgeon who does this very well."

"Is it something I need to do right away?" I asked.

"No. You can do it anytime when you are ready," he assured me.

I nodded, took the name and assured him that, when I was ready, I would go and talk to the surgeon. I thought, at that moment, that I would never be ready to do such a thing. It did take me several months to work up my courage to even make an appointment to talk to that surgeon. I finally convinced myself that a surgery such as this one might not be so bad. I would be put under some anesthetic, I was certain, so I wouldn't really know what they were doing, would I?

As my eyesight began to bother me more and more, and I had almost convinced myself to trust the surgeon, especially since I would be asleep and unaware, anyway, I made the appointment. My husband and I drove three hours to have a consultation in the big city.

The surgeon explained the procedure to me in much the same way that the young ophthalmologist had explained it. I had rehearsed it enough that it didn't even faze me. He asked if I had any further questions, and I said, "Well, I will be 'asleep', I suppose, so I…" and the surgeon broke in, "Oh no. You need to be awake for the surgery, but you won't feel anything. I need to have you conscious."

He and my husband entered into a discussion which distracted them from me and my reaction to this news. A few minutes later, after some very pleasant and cordial good-byes, a young woman came into the room in order to schedule the surgery.

I said that I would think it over and call back.

My husband said, "Maybe we had better schedule it. You have to get a pre-surgery appointment, too, with your GP, so this could be complicated. And, remember, the surgeon said that he is booked up for most of the summer already."

I hadn't heard any of this…shock, I think.

The girl began to offer dates, and I was still stuttering something about needing to think, but my husband picked two of the closest dates and then turned to me and said, "Which one?"

It was an old trick. I had used it on my children who didn't want to go to bed, "Do you want Fluffy or Grouchy with you tonight?" and while they decided, I would plop them into their cribs.

I picked the date that was earliest, because, later in that month, my youngest daughter was to return home after spending a year teaching in Korea, and I didn't want to be recuperating from surgery when she first got home. If I was recuperating. If I had had a surgery. I knew I could cancel this appointment. I made certain of that.

We waltzed out of that building, whistling a happy tune. I was happy to get out of there, and my husband thought that everything was just fine. He was surprised to hear me say to my son a few days later, "Oh, we made an appointment, but I think I'm going to cancel it!"

He couldn't understand why being awake as they put 'three little holes in the eye, flushed it out, and scraped the inside of it with a tiny little tool', might freak me out.

I finally did come to terms with the idea. I went over it again and again in my mind's eye. I finally realized that I did want to be able to see the world around me and that I had an opportunity that many people might not have.

We went to stay at my son's home in the city on the night before the surgery. I took a pirate's hat with me and our pet parrot. I told my grandchildren that I would be a real pirate when I came back from the surgery because I would have a patch over my eye.

We had to be at the surgery center before 6AM the next morning, but, strangely enough, my son and family had moved to a new home on the very same city street as the Center, and so this was not very intimidating. We drove right up the street about six blocks and turned into the parking lot. Two hours later I was awake with my head securely sandbagged, and my body tightly wrapped in a bundle, with my face lightly covered with a drape.

I had been given some type of anesthesia to prevent any pain or feeling at all. And my vision had been blocked somehow. As the surgery began, or when I thought it 'began', all I could see were the shadows of the surgeon and the nurse. I could hear them murmuring to each other. I could see only white swirls and the faint shadow people, and then a little black tool that moved in the white swirls…back and forth. My mind could barely conceive of the thought that I was seeing a tool inside my eye. Awesome.

As I lay there in wonder I felt a memory stirring. I had had an experience like this before somewhere. Then it came to me…

Once when I was a very little girl, I had gone over onto the courthouse lawn of the little town where we lived. There had been a parade and a concert, and I was tired of sitting with my parents and so I had run off with some other children to play in the evergreen bushes that surrounded the old stone edifice. At some point I had gotten an evergreen needle in my eye, and it burned and hurt. My father had managed to get the tiny green sliver out of my eye, but it still burned. Matty Cully, an old woman who lived around the corner from us and baked pies which she sold to the town restaurant for a living, was next to my parents, and when she heard my whimpers, she told my parents that she knew what to do.

She went home quickly and returned with a little glass bottle of cream. She made me lie down in the grass and tip my chin up a bit, then she held my burning eye open, and she poured the cool cream into it. Immediately, it stopped burning. The soothing coolness, the swirling whiteness…I remember staring up into the white swirls, and I stopped sobbing, because all the pain was gone…

Of course, it took a few days to recover from the epiretinal surgery. I have a picture of me with an eye patch, a pirate hat and our parrot.

Healing tears. I didn't believe in them when I first read 'Rapunzel'. Perhaps, I didn't fully believe in them even when I finally read the whole story many years later.

But, I believe in them now.

Made in the USA
Charleston, SC
01 October 2012